Alone

Alone

Gerard d'Aboville

Translated from the French by Richard Seaver

Introduction by Paul Theroux

Arcade Publishing • New York

FIRST ENGLISH-LANGUAGE EDITION

Aboville, Gerard d'.
  [Seul. English]
  Alone / Gerard d'Aboville ; translated from the French by Richard Seaver ; introduction by Paul Theroux.
    p. cm.
  ISBN 1-55970-218-4
  1. Aboville, Gerard d' — Journeys. 2. Sector (Boat) 3. North Pacific Ocean. I. Title.
G477.A2613 1993
910'.09644 — dc20   93-9842

Published in the United States by Arcade Publishing, Inc., New York

Distributed by Little, Brown and Company

10 9 8 7 6 5 4 3 2 1

PRINTED IN THE UNITED STATES OF AMERICA

Of all the creatures on the face of the earth, humans are those who adapt most easily, not only to the most extreme temperatures and climates but also to the most arduous conditions that life imposes on them.

— Henri de Montfried

To these words I would simply like to add that humans derive this capacity to adapt through a characteristic that is theirs alone: the ability to dream and to hope.

I dedicate this book to all those men and women for whom this adventure — this ocean voyage — may serve to re-kindle in their hearts a spark of hope.

— Gerard d'Aboville

Contents

Acknowledgments   ix

Introduction   xi

Prologue   1

Chapter 1:   With a Big Roll of Dreams
under My Arm   3

Chapter 2:   "Good Luck"   22

Chapter 3:   Ahead of Me, an Enormous Void . . .   51

Chapter 4:   "Rowboat Calling Okera"   65

Chapter 5:   With My Head in the Stars   79

Chapter 6:   And If All This Were Really Pointless   92

Chapter 7:   Survival   108

Chapter 8:   Typhoons   115

Chapter 9:   Indelibly Inscribed   124

CONTENTS

Chapter 10:   Do You See the Coastline?   140

Chapter 11:   The "Heavenly Bum"   156

Chapter 12:   One Second Longer . . .   166

Acknowledgments

I would like to thank the friends, colleagues, and business associates who helped make this adventure possible:

Sector Sport Watches • Transpac • Accastillage Diffusion • Air France • Air France Cargo • P.L.B. • Capitaine Cook • Eurest • Go Sport • P.N.B.

as well as:

Audiophase • All Nippon Airways • Jean Barret • B.N.P. Issy-les-Moulineaux • Cabinet de Clarens • Le Cercle de la Mer in Paris • Le Borgne Navy Yard • B. & B. Navy Yard • The Hydro Technique Company • C.R.M. • Damart • Dif Tours • Elite Marine • Fédération française des industries nautiques • F.F.S.A. • France Info • Garage Arcillon • Garbolino • Hertz • Hesnault • International Airfreight Services Co. • J.C.D. • Ken Club • Lestra Sport • Lyophal • Mat Equipement • Mecanorem • Nautix • Neste • O.I.P. • Plastimo • Port de Plaisance La Trinité-sur-Mer • Ramtonic • Regma Systèmes • Sail France • Semari • Société Ono • Sofomarin • Sony • T.B.S. • 3 M • Transparence Production • U.S. Coast Guard • Veillet International • The City of Issy-les-Moulineaux

ACKNOWLEDGMENTS

The French Embassy in Tokyo • The French Consulate in New York • The French Consulate in San Francisco • Tokyo Power Squadron • Astoria Maritime Museum

Laurent de Bartillat • Charlie Cronheim • Commander Blanvillain • Eddy Zimansky and his YL • Georges de Marrez • Dr. Chauve • Olivier de Kersauson • John Oakes • Bruno de La Barre

Christophe • Louis-Noël • Claude Arnoult • Jean-Claude Dufour • Thomas's Scooter • Benoît and Philippe • Béatrice • Pierre Yvan • Didier and François • Moze • Mr. and Mrs. Takasse • Yagi Mitsuru • Charles and Thibault • Laurence and François • Raymond • Philippe • Renaud • Sophie • Arnaud • Vincent • Nathalie "the wonderful," and so many others

And Cornélia, for her patience . . .

Introduction

When my French publisher, Robert Laffont, asked me whom in the whole of France I wished to meet I said, "D'Aboville," whose book *Seul* (*Alone*) had just appeared. The next day at a café in the shadow of Saint-Sulpice, I said to d'Aboville's wife, Cornélia, "He is my hero." She replied softly, with feeling, "Mine, too."

It is a commonplace that almost anyone can go to the moon: you pass a physical and NASA puts you in a projectile and shoots you there. It is perhaps invidious to compare an oarsman with an astronaut, but rowing across the Pacific Ocean alone in a small boat, as the Frenchman Gerard d'Aboville did in 1991, shows old-fashioned bravery. Yet even those of us who go on journeys in eccentric circles, simpler and far less challenging than d'Aboville's, seldom understand what propels us. Ed Gillet paddled a kayak sixty-three days from California to Maui a few years ago and cursed himself much of the way for not knowing why he was making such a reckless crossing. Astronauts have a clear, scientific motive, but adventurers tend to evade the awkward questions why.

D'Aboville was forty-six when he single-handedly rowed a 26-foot boat designed especially for this unique voyage from Japan to Washington State in 1991. He had previously (in 1980) rowed across the Atlantic, also from west to east, Cape Cod to Brittany. But the Atlantic was a piece of cake compared with his Pacific crossing, one of the most difficult and dangerous in the world. For various reasons, d'Aboville set out very late in the season and was caught first by heavy weather and finally by tumultuous storms — 40-foot waves and 80-miles-per-hour winds. Many times he was terrified, yet halfway through the trip — which had no stops (no islands at all in that part of the Pacific) — when a Russian freighter offered to rescue him, "I was not even tempted." He turned his back on the ship and rowed on. The entire crossing, averaging 7,000 strokes a day, took him 134 days. I wanted to ask him why he had taken this enormous personal risk.

D'Aboville, short and compactly built, is no more physically prepossessing than another fairly obscure and just as brave long-distance navigator, the paddler Paul Caffyn of New Zealand. Over the past decade or so, Caffyn has circumnavigated Australia, Japan, Great Britain, and his own New Zealand through the low pressure systems of the Tasman Sea in his 17-foot kayak.

In a memorable passage in his book, *The Dark Side of the Wave,* Caffyn is battling a horrible chop off the North Island and sees a fishing boat up ahead. He deliberately paddles away from the boat, fearing that someone on board will see his flimsy craft and ask him where he is going: "I knew they would ask me why I was doing it, and I did not have an answer."

I hesitated to spring the question on d'Aboville. I asked him first about his preparations for the trip. A native of Brittany, he had always rowed, he said. "We never used outboard motors — we rowed boats the way other children pedaled bicycles." Long ocean crossings interested him, too, because he loves to design highly specialized boats.

His Pacific craft was streamlined — it had the long seaworthy lines of a kayak and a high-tech cockpit with a roll-up canopy that could seal in the occupant in rough weather.

A pumping system, using seawater as ballast, was designed for righting the boat in the event of a capsize. The boat had few creature comforts but all necessities: a stove, a sleeping place, roomy hatches for dehydrated meals and drinking water. D'Aboville also had a video camera and filmed himself rowing, in the middle of nowhere, humming the Alan Jackson country-and-western song "Here in the Real World." D'Aboville sang it and hummed it for months but did not know any of the words, or indeed the title, until I recognized it on his video.

"That is a very hard question," he said, when I asked him why he had set out on this seemingly suicidal trip — one of the longest ocean crossings possible, at one of the worst times of the year. He denied that he had any death wish. "And it is not like going over a waterfall in a barrel." He had prepared himself well. His boat was well found. He is an excellent navigator. "Yes, I think I have courage," he said when I asked him point-blank whether he felt he was brave.

It was the equivalent, he said, of scaling the north face of a mountain, typically the most difficult ascent. But this lonely four-and-a-half-month ordeal almost ended in his death by drowning, when a severe storm lashed the Oregon-Washington coast as d'Aboville approached it, upside down, in a furious sea. The video of his last few days at sea, taken by a Coast Guard vessel, is so frightening that d'Aboville wiped tears from his eyes watching it with me. "At this time last year I was in the middle of it." He quietly ignored my questions about the 40-foot waves. Clearly upset at the memory, he said, "I do not like to talk about it."

"Only an animal does useful things," he said at last, after a long silence. "An animal gets food, finds a place to sleep, tries to keep comfortable. But I wanted to do something that was not useful — not like an animal at all. Something only a human being would do."

The art of it, he was saying — such an effort was as much esthetic as athletic. And that the greatest travel always contains within it the seeds of a spiritual quest, or else what's the point? The English explorer Apsley Cherry-Garrard would have agreed with this. He went to Antarctica with Scott in the ship *Terra Nova* and made a six-week crossing of a stretch of Antarctica in 1912, on foot, in the winter, when that polar region is dark all day and night, with a whipping wind and temperature of 80 below.

"Polar exploration is at once the cleanest and most isolated way of having a bad time which has been devised" are the first words of his narrative. On this trek, which gave him the title for his book, *The Worst Journey in the World,* he wrote: "Why do some human beings desire with such urgency to do such things: regardless of the consequences, voluntarily, conscripted by no one but themselves? No one knows. There is a strong urge to conquer the dreadful forces of nature, and perhaps to get consciousness of ourselves, of life, and of the shadowy workings of our human minds. Physical capacity is the only limit. I have tried to tell how, and when, and where. But why? That is a mystery."

But there is no conquering, d'Aboville says. *Je n'ai pas vaincu le Pacifique, il m'a laissé passer.* "I did not conquer the Pacific," he said afterward. "It let me go across."

Paul Theroux

Alone

They say that with the passage of time the worst memories have a way of turning into positive memories. I know that these will never change; they were, and will always remain, terrible and terrifying.

I'll never forget the many times the boat capsized, especially the one when it turned a complete somersault, throwing me against the bulkhead. Then, with my frayed nerves stretched to the breaking point, I kept waiting for the final blow, the blow that would end it all, and let out a primal scream, like some wild beast.

Nor will I ever forget those other times when I battled for my life, feeling my strength waning minute by minute. And the taste of seawater in my mouth, in my lungs. The taste of death.

And all that alone, alone, alone.

1

With a Big Roll of Dreams
under My Arm

I love to poke around in shipyards where boats are put out of commission and dismantled. The artifacts you often come across charm and bewitch me, and give me the same sort of pleasure as an adult that I experienced as a child exploring in our attic. Not to mention the added enjoyment I derive from such places simply because they thrust me into the midst of my abiding passion: boats and ships.

Ancient teak doors of the fore and aft gangways remind me of their counterparts on the old cargo ship on which I went around the world when I was twenty, closing the book on my youth and marking my passage into manhood. Massive portholes, with their heavy brass fittings and thick glass, their extraordinarily stout hinges, make me think of the cyclones I lived through in the Indian Ocean and the gigantic tidal waves that went head-to-head with those incredible winds. A tall, well-pitted smokestack is all my mind needs to conjure up a turn-of-the-century fishing boat laboring through the heavy swells of the North Sea.

It was in one of these demolition shipyards, not far from Anvers, Belgium, on one fine day in 1984, that my eye was drawn to a photograph, yellowed by the passage of time: a picture of a crew posing proudly in front of the gangway of a banana boat, their captain sporting a tropical pith helmet. . . . Also in the shipyard, between two straw

3

mattresses, lay a pile of navigation charts and another pile of pilot charts, both long out of date. Their only hope for survival, assuming the mice did not get to them first, was to be reborn as recycled paper.

Pilot charts are large documents on which are plotted — and superimposed on corresponding navigational charts — statistical information concerning prevailing winds, ocean currents, paths taken by cyclones in a given area, and other such capricious meteorological data. After a great deal of rummaging through the Anvers shipyard, I managed to put together a full collection of the pilot charts for the North Pacific — that is, twelve, a chart for each month. I then headed back to Paris with a big roll of dreams under my arm.

At that point, I had absolutely no idea that I might one day set out to row across the Pacific Ocean. Four years earlier, in my successful conquest of the Atlantic, I had given my all, both physically and mentally, and had called on everyone I knew to help make it happen. In the course of that adventure — or, more precisely, that ordeal — which lasted seventy-two days, I thought I had pushed my abilities to the limit. Not to mention that I had doubtless used up a fair amount of my reserve of luck, since in the course of that crossing my boat, the *Captain Cook,* had capsized no fewer than five times.

Every now and then I would think about those North Pacific charts, take them down, and pore over them — at first out of a sense of curiosity more than anything else. But I knew I was playing with fire, and before long I had taken the final, inevitable step: I switched from dreaming to thinking. Now, if I ever *were* to do it, this is how I would go about it. . . .

To cross an ocean with a pair of oars as his only means of propulsion, the navigator has to be constantly aware of the prevailing winds as well as the ocean currents, which generally are related to those winds. There is no way any rowboat, especially one with a heavy cargo on board, can prevail against the winds and the power of the sea. Thus, the point of departure and the route to be taken are decisive.

For the Pacific, the longest route but also the most "comfortable" for a rowboat, or even a small sailboat, would be from east to west. Departing from either California or Mexico, the aim would be to pick up the trade winds as soon as possible, for the simple reason that the trade winds are fairly reliable and move in a favorable direction, storms are few and far between, and the climate is pleasant.

Such an east-to-west crossing, by rowing, was successfully undertaken in 1982 by the Englishman Peter Bird, who departed from San Francisco and arrived ten months later in Australia. But my idea, which was slowly beginning to take shape, was to do what I had done for the Atlantic — that is, row from west to east, across the northern Pacific. There the movement of barometric low pressure systems and frequent high winds held the promise of a potentially faster crossing. On the other side of that coin, I knew the sea would be much rougher — and far more dangerous. For me, it was the maritime equivalent of scaling the north face of some mighty mountain.

Years went by. I went back to sailing. I crossed the China Sea on a tiny racing catamaran. Then, having discovered in the Philippines the world's most extraordinary nautical paradise, I organized a series of long-distance catamaran races. Here, the adventure for me was making sure the course was plotted correctly and that the logistical support for two hundred competitors was forthcoming during the three weeks that they were totally on their own. Meanwhile, on the top shelf of my office, almost beyond reach, my antique charts awaited their appointed hour.

1990: A feeling that I was not getting any younger, a general sense of wear and tear on mind and body, business ventures that had turned sour, plus, I had to admit, an overall feeling of boredom. I vaguely knew that I needed to cleanse my mind, refocus my priorities, engage in some real combat. A combat in which I would invest all the daring, tenacity, and courage I could muster; all my considerable experience; all my profound knowledge of the sea. A combat into which I would throw myself body and soul, its success dependent solely upon me.

On my table, the pile of charts was now spread out before me.

By the fall of 1990, I still had not told anyone about my idea of rowing across the Pacific. Yet the idea had solidly taken hold. In my leisure moments, I found myself making rough sketches of the boat I had in mind. One of my friends, Louis-Noël, told me about a Swiss company, Sector, which manufactures sports watches. The firm's motto is "No Limits" — they champion the twin virtues of challenge and pushing yourself to the limit. The company's directors were always on the lookout for people with an international reputation who could concretely illustrate their motto and principles. Sector was already well entrenched in both the American and Japanese markets and was about to launch its products in the French market. I had a feeling Sector was tailor-made for me.

But let's not fool ourselves. How many times had I

thought I'd found the ideal sponsor, from the Atlantic crossing to the catamaran races in the China Sea, from the Paris-
to-Dakar race to the ocean-going yawl regattas, only to
discover that "your project is not quite right for us." The
step from a friendly word of encouragement from a potential sponsor — "Say, that sounds like a great idea!" — to
the actual signing of a contract is a very big one. A step
that both my friend Christopher, a seasoned automobile
driver, and Saint Christopher himself, patron saint of all
seasoned drivers, helped me take, each in his own way.

Let me introduce Christopher by describing his relationship to his car, and to driving in general. The easiest
way to describe Christopher's automobile is to say that the
Fiat 500 is without a doubt the least aggressive car on the
road. A tiny, two-passenger vehicle, it has a rounded, non-
threatening design, a motor that can only be described as
ridiculous, an overall appearance that is midway between
old-fashioned and user-friendly. This toy car makes the
most prejudiced pedestrians feel well inclined toward it,
causes other drivers to regard it with bemused conde-
scension, and inspires ardent ecologists to cite it as a prime
example of a generally reprehensible species. Despite all
this, when Christopher got behind the wheel of his Fiat
500, this innocent little vehicle metamorphosed into a
guided missile. Woe to anyone who got in its way! Any
other driver became an incongruity, any pedestrian a plain
nuisance, any sharp curve in the road a godsend, any po-
liceman a sworn enemy. With Christopher driving his Fiat
500, the most tranquil village square was immediately
transformed into a universe in which any sense of pity —
in fact, any human feeling at all — was no longer tolerated.

Within this universe, the worst position was that of the
poor passenger. Separated from a world that had suddenly
turned hostile by only a thin sheet of metal, all a passenger
could do was make himself smaller, sinking down deeper

in his seat and hoping by this act of self-contraction not only to protect himself against angry looks from all sides but to prepare himself for the ultimate collision.

Christopher was twenty-six, a bachelor, and had the physique of a Greek god. Girls swooned as soon as they laid eyes on him. His only problem in that department was an embarrassment of riches, and his plan seemed to be to maintain that status quo as long as possible. If a girlfriend became a trifle too clinging, he would bundle her into "The Pimple," the name he gave to his little Fiat meteor, and take her for a spin around the Place de l'Etoile. For anyone who has never had the experience of trying to circumnavigate the Place de l'Etoile in Paris, know that, with its eight impinging side streets, its lack of police direction, its presumed "priority" to the right,* and its inherent challenge to French drivers, it has to be — even for a so-called competent driver — one of the most dangerous intersections on the face of the earth. A little ride around L'Etoile usually sufficed to straighten out the young lady. Better a life without Christopher than face certain death with him, she would say to herself. Having come to that sad conclusion, she would then hop out of the Fiat and head home to her parents. By subway.

But for the moment, let us leave aside the private life of my friend Christopher — which could well be the subject of a separate volume, the title of which, you can be sure, would not be *Alone* — and focus on the professional life of this breaker-of-hearts and stripper-of-gears.

Christopher had helped me organize the catamaran races in the China Sea. Now that the event was over, he, like me, was temporarily unemployed.

I had talked to him about the Pacific project, and it

---

* In France, a basic rule of the road is that the car coming from the right has the right of way. — *Tr.*

excited him enormously. In contrast to my Atlantic adventure, this time I had decided I would do things right: plan meticulously, be totally professional, formulate a complete plan from the start with a would-be sponsor, and either put myself in charge or at least direct the tightly knit team I would put together. I needed someone who could make key decisions for me in my absence, who could handle crises without panicking, who would know exactly what to do if, for example, I were out of communication with the rest of the world for several weeks. In short, I needed someone in whom I had complete confidence. In Christopher, I believed I had found my ideal person. In addition to his native intelligence, he was blessed with a great sense of humor — a quality that served him in good stead during the trying times we lived through during the long months prior to my departure.

I must also confess that, above and beyond any rational or logical considerations for my choice of Christopher as point man, it did occur to me more than once that if I had survived my many trips with him through the streets of Paris, aboard his mini-meteor, I also had to believe that it was destiny's way of telling me I was meant to survive any future ordeal.

Christopher and I made contact with Sector and set up an appointment at their offices in Lausanne, Switzerland. Our train left at dawn, and we set off for the station on a motorcycle in a driving rain. (NEVER DO THINGS THE EASY WAY has to be my motto.) By the time we found our compartment on the train, we were so drenched we had to strip to our shorts and hang up our clothes to dry. When we arrived at the Swiss border, I discovered to my dismay that in my hurried, predawn departure, I had neglected to take my passport. In desperation, I pulled out an old issue of *Paris Match*, which had reported, in text and photos, my Atlantic crossing. The customs official looked at the photos, studied my face closely, reexamined the pictures, then gruffly acknowledged that with the exception of the slightly receding hairline, I was indeed who I claimed to be. "Still and all," he murmured as he fingered the magazine, "a passport's a lot more practical identity card than a copy of *Paris Match*."

Our meeting with the Sector people went well; they seemed excited by the project, and we left feeling we were definitely on the right track.

People often have the wrong idea about corporate sponsorship of sports figures or sporting events. Companies that, by their product or approach to business, seem the most progressive generally turn out to be the most exacting, demand the most meticulous preparation and professional team, and, as a result, the most detailed budgets. For anyone not blessed with a personal fortune, corporate sponsors are the only way that most sports projects ever see the light of day.

Generally speaking, sponsors of sporting events work in either of two ways (or a combination of both) when it comes to publicity. The more conventional route is for a company to ally itself to the sporting event or personality through billboards or television spots. The second approach is to associate directly with the person or event, as is often the case, say, when tennis stars wear a sponsor's clothing or use its rackets, or when basketball stars display their gargantuan talents shod in a sponsor's shoes. With the first route — billboards and television spots — the results are to some degree predictable, therefore measurable. With the second, personal relations come into play; that is, there is a closer connection between the sports personality and the sponsor, a basic harmony created between the image of the personality and the sponsoring party. There is also a greater risk — the possibility that a sports star may not live up to expectations or that the sponsored event turns sour. In our case, we stressed the positive market aspects of our proposed voyage and Sector's own market — what I call the Japan–United States–France connection. We also pointed out that not only was the watch the basic instrument of navigation but that the voyage would stress their product's durability, its ability to survive the most extreme conditions, et cetera. From Sector's viewpoint, they had to assess the risks of my project and gauge its chances of success. If the crossing were successful, they would doubtless recoup their investment many times over.

We compiled extensive files, had further discussions, added more documents to our files, and reached a point where a draft contract was drawn up. Then the Gulf War erupted and all advertising seemed to dry up as the world focused, for weeks and weeks, on Iraq, Kuwait, and the volatile tension in that part of the world. It would take more than optimism for any sponsor to give the green light to a project that seemed at best peripheral given the world conditions. Even under normal conditions, a project as difficult and ambitious as ours was not a foregone conclusion for any sponsor. I was ultimately an unknown factor to the Sector people, and, our convincing presentation aside, the enterprise was in fact quite foreign to them. To underwrite it was a considerable risk, a real leap of faith.

Despite everything, the contract did get signed. All my demands were met: I would be solely responsible for the nautical aspect of the enterprise, for picking my team, for the materials, for the choice of a shipyard where the boat would be built, for the date of departure, and for the film that would be made of the voyage. Sector also agreed — and I confess I had not expected them to — that there would be a minimum of prepublicity. No brass bands. No banners or streamers. And as for the name of my boat, instead of plain *Sector*, they could have insisted on something more commercial, such as *Sector Sportswatches*, especially since in France at that time no one even knew that Sector manufactured watches. They did manage to let it be known that they were sponsoring me, but they did it discreetly and with great elegance. Throughout, Sector would display the same class act.

Above all, I needed a boat perfectly adapted to the demands of the voyage, one that would resemble no other boat ever built. Nothing you could find in any boat builder's catalogue. I had already made up my mind who should build it: my old friend, Bernard Fournier Le Ray.

Bernard and I had worked together designing and constructing the boat I had rowed across the Atlantic. Since those pioneering days, Bernard had opened a shipyard at La Trinité-sur-Mer in Brittany. He is the best in the business, a kind of wizard of far-out prototypes. When it comes to boats, I am something of a perfectionist — a finicky perfectionist, if that is not a redundancy — a quality for which I trust I'll be forgiven, when you consider how I use my boats. As for *Sector*, it was imperative to have complete confidence in the team responsible for its construction. Bernard, meticulous to a fault, is also impeccable when it comes to schedules, which is rare in his profession. When I first mentioned my project to him at the end of December 1990, his response was a categorical no. He had more orders than he could fill, and there was no way he could fit another project into his schedule. I knew that Bernard, who never wanted to take a job he couldn't deliver on time, had a tendency to react negatively to any potential new order in an effort to discourage the prospective client. I had seen him do it more than once, but I also knew my Bernard. At the end of January I raised the subject again. When his answer this time was "That's a tall order, my friend," I knew the battle was won. At the beginning of March work got underway.

Until now I had kept my family in the dark about the project. My wife, Cornélia, knew that this is the kind of decision I make on my own and that any effort to talk me out of it would be pointless. To have brought the subject up any sooner, while it was still no more than an idea I was mulling over, would have worried her prematurely and unnecessarily. Having sailed the seven seas with me and experienced the worst conditions possible, she knew exactly what such an endeavor meant: it would never even have crossed my mind to minimize the dangers. When I told her I realized the trip would be hard, very hard, she knew precisely what I meant by that word.

Cornélia accepted my announcement, not only because of her intelligence — that is, a superior form of understanding — but first and foremost because she backed my project wholeheartedly. My children, Guillaume and Ann, aged fifteen and ten respectively, each reacted in their own way: Guillaume, like me an introvert, kept his feelings to himself, whereas Ann shut herself in her room and sobbed her heart out. In the months and years to come, I was to learn that this adventure was an ordeal not only for me but perhaps even more for my family.

An egotist? There's no denying I am one. But would I do better to give my children the example of a father who, faced with the possibility of pushing himself to the limit, even at the risk of losing his life, shrank back and said no?

In April, I spent a week in Japan scouting the coastline for potential points of departure. I finally settled on the port of Choshi. Less than sixty miles from Tokyo, and even closer to the Tokyo airport, Choshi is situated at the extremity of a promontory, a kind of nose pointing seaward, toward the east, my direction. By departing from Choshi, I would avoid all the dangerous harbor traffic both in the bay of Tokyo and the port of Yokohama, which would improve my chances of gaining the high seas without an untoward encounter with a steamship or trawler.

Back in Paris, I held a press conference to announce officially my planned Pacific crossing. The press conference was held at the *Cercle de la Mer*, the Maritime Center, and the journalists who had been invited were handed a map of the Pacific Ocean, on one side of which was printed:

> September 20, 1980. Upon his arrival after having rowed across the Atlantic, Gerard d'Aboville declared: "If there is one thing I can say with utter conviction, it is that never again will I set out on any such slave-ship!"

On the other side was printed this statement:

> Paris, April 24, 1991. "If there is one thing I've learned, it is that one can never be sure of anything or anybody, most of all oneself."

Eleven years earlier, in the same circumstances and virtually in the same spot, my announcement that I intended to row alone across the Atlantic from west to east had stunned the audience. Looking around the room, I recognized a number of faces. In the eleven intervening years, no one had grown any younger. Barely had that thought crossed my mind when I realized that they must be thinking exactly the same thing about me.

May came and went. It's a catastrophic month in France, when nothing gets done. Long weekends with holidays at one end or the other — or both. There are also holidays in the middle of the week, which prompts people to sneak in a vacation day or two and eliminate the workweek entirely. It's as though the country closes down for a whole month. But not for Bernard, who was working with his team around the clock to make sure he brought the boat in on schedule. We were constantly on the phone as he asked me for one piece of equipment or another: this or that part of the superstructure, the solar panels, the batteries, on and on.

Sector began to take shape. It was being made with the most advanced composite materials available. For the hull and deck, Bernard was using a special foam 15 millimeters thick (about half an inch), which had the virtue of being nonabsorbent even when it was totally immersed. That material was sandwiched between two carbon fiber layers, each less than a millimeter thick.

The solid-cast material had the paradoxical virtue of being at once absolutely rigid and extremely strong as well as very light, but it had one major drawback: once built, there was no question of drilling a hole into it, or adding a screw or two in the event you discovered you needed some additional support or reinforcement. That is why Bernard had to know from the very start of construction exactly what accessories would be required, not only on the upper surface of the boat but below deck and in the cockpit.

But May almost did us in. Bernard was counting on us to come up with all the equipment and accessories in a timely manner, so from our offices on the outskirts of Paris, Christopher and I spent endless hours on the phone trying to track down the parts we needed, growing increasingly angry with each call. Either no one was in the office or the managers — the only ones who could make the decision — were out of town or unavailable. When would the boss be available? Oh, not until next Tuesday at the earliest. But

15

didn't he leave any instructions? The item was supposed to be ready last week. No, sorry, I can't seem to find any information about the part you ordered. Why don't you try again next week. Next week? I can't wait until next week!

The days sped by, and with each one our nerves grew more frayed and our frustration mounted. The hours spent on the phone kept me from the physical training program I had designed for myself. It is true that my project did not require a particularly muscular person. Not even a world-class athlete — which I am not. But I did have to be in perfect health. I had to feel comfortable that nothing medically serious would happen to me during the next six months, when I would be far from any hospital or doctor. This is why, on May 21, I found myself in the Cochin hospital in Paris, my entire body crisscrossed from one end to the other, in a manner I can only describe as indiscreet, with various and sundry microscopically small tubes at the ends of which were attached miniature cameras. The most fascinating part of that examination was watching the television screen as those tiny cameras probed my inner being.

I would gladly have forgone that intimate and highly original examination, but, at forty-five, there was a fair chance that the old carcass might conceal some minor, or even major, breakdown that had not yet revealed itself to the world. Luckily, I left the hospital with the blessings of Dr. Boissionas ringing in my ears: "No apparent problems. You're declared fit for service."

Meanwhile, Bernard had put the finishing touches to his newborn: as it left the shipyard, *Sector* looked sleek and beautiful.

I will not dwell overly on the technical aspects of the boat, except to provide the reader with a general description, which can be supplemented with a closer look at the detailed diagram on pages 18 and 19.

Sector was eight meters in length — about twenty-six feet — and 1.6 meters, or about five feet, wide. It weighed 250 kilos empty, and 650 when fully loaded — that is, about 600 pounds empty and about 1,500 pounds fully loaded. It consisted of three compartments:

- in the stern: a watertight cabin, my living quarters
- midships: an open cockpit, my rowing quarters
- in the bow: also watertight, the storage area

We loaded *Sector* on a trailer and headed for our family house in Kérantré, Brittany. The boat's travels began with a ceremony that for me at least was completely unanticipated. My mother had asked me in passing if I would mind having a few neighbors drop by to see the boat, a request I had readily granted.

Scarcely had *Sector* landed on the family property than out of nowhere there appeared a contingent of faith commandos. The chaplain of the local seminary led the way, and, in his wake, was a tight little pack of very determined nuns. Weapons and munitions were revealed without further ado: aspergillum at the ready, an ice bucket next to it half filled with holy water. Before I could say or do anything, *Sector* — in my opinion completely free of original sin — was the victim of a very proper and official baptism.

Not wholly convinced of the magical properties of the operation that had just taken place, and slightly irritated by the unexpected nature of the ceremony, which had all the earmarks of being well planned, I nonetheless decided to accept it gracefully: if nothing else during the coming months, it would help my parents sleep better while I was out at sea.

The rest of the holy water was poured over the roots of

1 Forward peak

2 Watertight bulkhead

3 Forward stabilizer housing

4 Forward stabilizer

5 Storage area for oars

6 Storage area for provisions

7 Telex antenna

8 Solar panels

9 Oarlocks

10 Saltwater filter

11 Built-in desalination pump

12 Rowing seat

13 Port ballast

14 Compass

15 Radio antenna

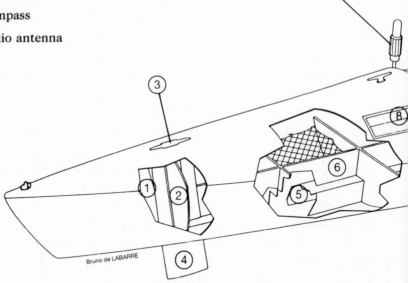

Bruno de LABARRE

18

16 Gas stove

17 Rudder control mechanism

18 Speed log

19 Portholes that can be opened

20 Bunk

21 Pump for transferring seawater

22 Saltwater transfer gates

23 Portside porthole

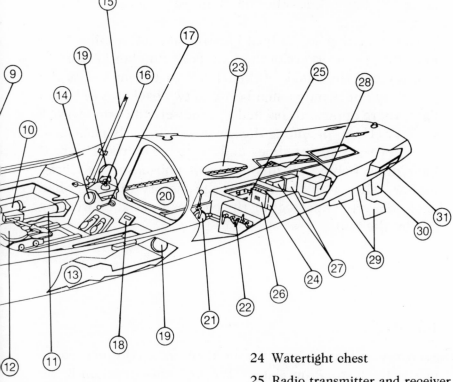

24 Watertight chest

25 Radio transmitter and receiver

26 Telex chest

27 Nickel-cadmium batteries chest

28 Electrical distribution chest

29 Aft stabilizers

30 Rudder blade

31 Aft ballast

19

a massive camellia shrub, so I thought it worthwhile upon my return home to check and see what effect, if any, the holy water had had on it. On the basis of the evidence, I think I can safely state that, while it is far from certain that the holy water had any beneficial effect, I am pleased to report that it clearly had no negative effect. Later, comparing the shrub carefully to its neighboring camellias, I can assert that I detected no noticeable increase in its size or flower, but on the other hand, no suspicious diminution either.

The same day as the boat blessing and a few miles from Kérantré, the workers of the Ono Pork Butcher Factory in Pontivy had the shock of their lives. At the far end of the assembly line, sandwiched between two packages of baked ham, there appeared, packed in precisely the same way, a sweater. Then, in among the sausages, similarly packaged, were several pairs of shoes and some tee shirts. The brilliant mind behind all this apparent nonsense was Christopher, who, with the help of the factory manager, had devised a way of protecting the clothes I would be wearing during the trip.

June 16

Sector was loaded into the hold of an Air France cargo plane. Its destination: Japan. We were due to rejoin it the following day. I was still very concerned about all the time we had lost in May. And worried about the possibilities of further delays — Japan is such a complicated country. Cornélia, Guillaume, and Ann accompanied me to the airport. I'm not what you might call a very effusive person when it comes to good-byes. Nor in any other circumstances, I might add.

All of us put up a good front, keeping our emotions at bay by exchanges of light-hearted banter. Were they fully aware of the potential consequences of what I was about to do? Or, for that matter, was I?

2

"Good Luck"

June 17

As our plane descended toward Narita Airport on the outskirts of Tokyo, I had only one thought in mind: put out
to sea as soon as possible. For the past six months, all I'd
done was negotiate and argue with suppliers, bureaucrats,
and backers. All the delays in building and fitting out the
boat had completely worn me out.

My most optimistic projections had convinced me that
the northern Pacific route would take from four to five
months. My original plan, therefore, had been to leave
Japan in the spring, with the hope of reaching the California
coastline early in the fall. I knew that after October the
weather conditions in the North Pacific changed dramati-
cally for the worse: storms are more frequent, last much
longer, the seas are extremely rough — especially dangerous for small craft — and, certainly not the least to consider, the days grow shorter and colder.

Even back in Paris, I was obsessed with having to postpone my departure date. I was undertaking not only a test
of endurance but a race against the clock. At issue was not
just success or failure in the usual sense of terms — my
life was on the line.

Now as we touched down at Narita, I opened my 1991
desk diary and duly noted the entry under June 2: *Possible*

departure date. At the time I'd made that entry, it seemed a reasonable assumption for a crazy project, but it did not take into account two elements: the Gulf War and the impossible month of May in France. The former I could not have foreseen, but from long experience I should have anticipated problems during that spring month of national paralysis. We were already two weeks behind schedule — was there any chance we might make up some of that lost time here in Japan?

My first official task was to visit the naval authorities of the port of Choshi. Accompanying me was my faithful guide and interpreter, Mitsuru. We left our shoes at the door and precariously made our way across an impeccably polished linoleum floor toward a group of functionaries seated at a table at the far end of the room. There were six in all, and to me it looked as we approached that all six were shaking their heads in unison, doubtless wondering how they were going to deal with this crazy Frenchman and his cockeyed project: Had they understood correctly? He was going to cross the Pacific by *rowing?* If in the rest of the world my project had met with either a show of surprise or skepticism, here in Japan, where individual exploits are uncommon, where group decisions are the rule, not the exception, where long communal discussions are required before any major decision is made, on any level of the multilayered hierarchy, it ran into a stone wall of incomprehension.

I told them that my boat, the *Sector*, would be arriving shortly in Japan, which provoked a round of murmurs among my bureaucratic sextet, all of whom seemed visibly embarrassed. Sensing that language or customs might be a barrier, I had come armed with a model of the boat and its equipment. I was sure that a simple show-and-tell would be far more eloquent and convincing than any words I could

23

muster. I showed them the model, complete with tiny oars, and thought I had convinced them of the nature and validity of the project, when I realized from Mitsuru's translation that at least one of these gentlemen had thought I was the *builder* of the model boat and was seeking authorization to sail it in the Choshi port. Adding to the confusion was an electronic device I showed them, which they took to be the radar command for the toy boat. When I explained to them that this was my distress signal, which I would wear day and night throughout the voyage, it provoked an avalanche of technical questions that I tried to field as best I could. The more authoritative I sounded, I thought, the better my chances of success.

Who among them would break rank and offer a personal opinion? Without any rules or regulations to fall back on, all functionaries, in my experience, no matter what their nationality, are almost always thrown for a loss.

While the two lower-rung bureaucrats in the room buried themselves in their eternal files, their superiors withdrew in pairs into their inner chambers to continue their consultations. It was ten minutes to six, and I knew the offices closed at six sharp. It was a critical situation, because the next day I was slated to be in Tokyo for a press conference. The unsmiling gentlemen filed back into the room, and it was clear to me that either no decision had been made or, if it had, the news was not good. Smiling, I greeted them with my ace in the hole, a photo album, including press coverage, of my 1980 Atlantic crossing, to show them both the nature and seriousness of my project. It was a propitious decision, for I could see that not only did they now understand but that I had offered the leader of the group a way out of the impasse without losing face.

"And when you left the United States, what did the American authorities say to you?"

"They said to me, 'Good luck!' "

A new retreat into private chambers by all six. A minute later one of them reappeared, smiling broadly, and said: "We say to you, 'Good luck!' "

June 18

Back in Tokyo. Sector's agent, Jack Sagazaki, had done a first-rate job on the press conference. The room was packed with journalists and, in addition, the French ambassador had graced the event with his presence, which lent the project an authoritative air that it needed badly.

During the introductory remarks, which were going on forever, I thought back to the press conference we had held in Paris a few weeks before. We had carefully placed the personal representative of the Japanese ambassador to France in the front row. The next day I called him to request, now that he presumably understood the project, that he write a letter of introduction for me to the pertinent authorities in Japan, explaining both the nature and importance of the project. After a long pause on the other end — it was probably no more than ten seconds but seemed like a half hour — he answered, in obvious embarrassment, "I'm so very sorry, but there's nothing I can do. Just think, what if everybody decided to do what you're doing! And besides, this is something I clearly must discuss with my colleagues. . . ."

I had gotten my first lesson in the mentality of the Japanese bureaucrat.

Francesco Iacono, Sector's marketing director for worldwide sales, explained why his company was sponsoring the event. Then he passed the microphone to me.

As I had in Paris, I began by showing the route I planned to take, explaining the reasons for the northern choice and for picking Japan as my point of departure. I also ran through the communication devices I had on board, the solar-operated radio and the telex that would communicate via satellite. Then I gave a thorough rundown on *Sector* itself, using my well-worn model and its basic equipment. After that I said I'd be happy to answer any questions.

"Where is your toilet?"

"Excuse me?"

"I mean, on your model I don't see any indication of either a shower or toilet? Could you tell us where they are, or how you're going to handle . . . ah . . . those things?"

Slightly taken aback by the completely unexpected question, in good French fashion, I tried a diversionary tactic, hoping humor would win the day.

"Well, the fact is, the toilet is all around the boat."

Since my questioner seemed not at all enlightened by my response, I pressed on, not realizing that humor has no place in matters of such gravity and substance.

"You might say that I will be the first transpacific traveler who will be rowing through his own cesspool."

Now I sensed that the more I said the worse things would get and, fearing that my words, especially in translation, could have catastrophic repercussions on the ecological front, I finished with a flourish, hoping to repair the damage.

"I should also add that I will be the first transpacific traveler who, thanks to my desalination pumps, will be drinking water for five months from his cesspool."

Muted laughter from that part of the room where the French journalists were gathered; total bafflement everywhere else. (That evening a major Japanese tabloid would publish a lovely sketch of the *Sector* — its shower and toilet prominently displayed!)

Another question: "When do you expect to leave?"

"As soon as I've had a chance to check out all the equipment and the weather turns favorable."

"I see. Which means when, exactly?"

For a moment I had forgotten that we were in Japan, where it is inconceivable for any project to be taken seriously unless its timetable has been rigorously projected.

"Well, uh, I should say . . . June twenty-third!"

June 19

The various people scheduled either to work with me on the project or cover it for the media were slowly arriving. The video crew. The photographer. The journalist from French television. And, none too soon, Bruno.

I had known Bruno for almost thirty years. He had helped me design and build the *Captain Cook* in the late 1970s, and he had rejoined my crew in Brittany for the launching and testing of the *Sector*. He had followed me to Japan to make sure the new boat would be functioning perfectly when I set out.

Bruno's knowledge of all things nautical was phenomenal. He was a walking encyclopedia; he could answer any question having to do with ships and boats, ancient or modern, whether it was the overall length of the piping on a nuclear submarine or the meaning of the word *chafuste*.* He could tell you in a trice the weight of the *Normandie*'s propellers — or the age of its last captain.

More important, his practical knowledge was as great as his theoretical knowledge, and in nautical matters he tolerated no compromise on any front. His passion for the

---

* Archaic, and quite rare, French nautical term for steam engine.

sea was such, in fact, that he often ran into difficulties with the land-based police, who tended to show abysmal ignorance when it came to maritime matters. For instance, Bruno's car had been stopped more than once simply because the vehicle was outfitted — like any boat worthy of its name — with green lights to starboard and red lights to port.

No sooner had he landed in Japan than Bruno showed his true colors. His traveling companions suggested that he go up to Tokyo with them, where they were scheduled to meet Christopher and me. "Sorry, guys," was his answer. "I came here to take care of *Sector*, which is due to arrive today. I'll be at the airport to meet it."

They pointed out to him that while *Sector* might indeed be arriving that day, it would be kept in a warehouse somewhere in customs. In which case, Bruno responded, "I'll stay in the warehouse with it. I brought my sleeping bag, so that won't be a problem." Notified by phone of Bruno's adamant stance, Christopher used all his considerable powers of persuasion to convince our walking encyclopedia that after fifteen hours of air travel he could profit from a few hours sleep without jeopardizing *Sector*'s future.

June 20

The customs officials at Narita Airport were perplexed. My freeze-dried food concentrate — all 120 kilos of it, or about 250 pounds — had just arrived, and these officials, food specialists all, could not for the life of them figure out into which category the material should fall. Importing food into Japan is tightly controlled, and they would doubtless have to open every aluminum-sealed package to verify its contents. Each package, by the way, contained a single dish.

I explained to the number one customs official that were he to do so, the food would be ruined, which would mean abandoning my project. Nonetheless I did open one package. He poured the mummified contents onto the table. He stared at it for a long moment, then looked up at me, looked down again at the "food," then said to me, clearly in a state of disbelief, "You mean to say you're going to eat *this* for five months?"

I told him that when you added a little hot water to what he saw before him, it turned magically into a juicy steak.

Gingerly, he put the dried steak back into its container. As he went about signing the customs forms, he asked us, in an apparent cultural aside, how the French ate their steaks, and what side dishes went best with them, in our opinion. As we left, I noted that he had put on his teapot to boil. Just add a little hot water, you say?

Having taken care of these formalities, Mitsuru, Christopher, and I set out for Choshi by car, followed by *Sector* on a flatbed truck, with Bruno baby-sitting right beside it. As soon as the convoy arrived, Bruno set about preparing *Sector* for its Far-Eastern launching. Dear Bruno. Until the day I set off, he left *Sector*'s side only when he was forced to run some absolutely indispensable errand. He slept on board. He kept a round-the-clock check on its mooring lines. He checked and rechecked its fittings, constantly coming up with suggestions for improvements, to the point where his sense of perfection began to get on my nerves. But how many times, in the course of that interminable voyage at sea, did I think back with gratitude and wonder at the care and concern he had lavished on this frail craft, and thank him silently for some fitting or fixture which, because of him, functioned perfectly.

June 21

The rest of the crew were due to rejoin us from Tokyo. They weren't exactly sure of their arrival time, because on their way they had to pick up an indispensable piece of video equipment we had forgotten to bring from France. One tiny piece of equipment and five healthy, reasonably sane adults — what could be simpler? Six hours later, they finally showed up. Wiped out and in a state of nervous exhaustion bordering on hysteria, they explained that they had gotten lost, not once, not a dozen times, but repeatedly, endlessly. Their only satisfaction was that they had found the missing piece of equipment. That was the good news. The bad news was that they had left it in the last taxi they had taken! To make matters worse, it had not stopped raining since we arrived. The rain didn't stop our progress, but it did dampen our fragile morale. One did not need a crystal ball to know that my trials and tribulations had only begun.

The Riverside Hotel, where we were staying, was not exactly what one would call a palace. The intrepid traveler was greeted by a floor covering not of wool carpet but of a kind of plastic matting, bright green in color, like an artificial lawn.

The beds were a mite small, which had a certain virtue in that, had they been standard length, they would have spilled out into the hallway, and had they been any wider, the room would have been wall-to-wall bed. From the hotel's name, one might infer that, in contrast to the minor drawbacks, the weary voyager would at least have a lovely view of the Tone River. Not so. Between the hotel and the lemon-colored waters of the river stood another building, its wall a scant ten feet from our windows.

On the other hand, the prices at the Riverside were quite

reasonable, in a country where prices in general approached the astronomical.

Anyway, all this was of little importance, since we would be staying at the hotel only for a few days at the most.

The shakedown cruise had gone well, and the only items remaining to be verified were the radio and telex.

I had outfitted *Sector* with two complementary types of communication. The radio, which was similar to the one I had used crossing the Atlantic eleven years before, enabled me to communicate with ham radio operators as well as with maritime stations that maintained phone communication among naval vessels of all kinds.

Radio contact with both of these groups was as essential as it was seductive, but it had two drawbacks. For one, the radio used a fair amount of electricity, especially considering the rather complicated calling procedure before you could make contact with the outside world. The other drawback was the chance nature of wavelengths, which obliged the sender to juggle frequencies that varied according to one's position at sea, the time of day, and so forth. It would therefore be impossible to establish contact with any certainty, and the contacts that were made could be cut off at any time.

This was where the telex came in. It came equipped with a mini-computer on which one could both write and receive messages. Its antenna was designed to be kept in the "up" position at all times, but, given the constant risk of capsizing, I intended to lower it after every use. The telex would send a message to a satellite, which would relay it to the nearest station on earth, and from there it could be retransmitted anywhere in the world.

That apparatus had the dual advantage of reducing to a

minimum the length of a transmission, thereby consuming only a small amount of electricity, and of not requiring someone on the other end to receive the message at the time it was sent. I was counting on the telex to serve as backup to my radio contacts in the event that for any reason I couldn't get through.

The beauty of having the two systems — radio and telex — on board was that they were completely independent from each other. Both systems had been tested in France and found satisfactory. Not so here in the Far East. Try as we would, we could not get either system to work.

No longer any question of leaving in two days — it was back to the drawing board!

June 23

Upon arriving this morning at the boat, I realized how foolish I had been to blurt out a departure date at the press conference. I had denied a dozen times over that I had ever set such a firm date, but no one seemed to believe me. Everybody was there: the sponsor's representative, the television crews, the photographers, and — worst of all — the Japanese officials who had left Tokyo at the crack of dawn to make sure they didn't miss the historic event. Poor Bruno was surrounded, fielding a veritable barrage of questions. But the key, constant refrain was:

"When, please, will the departure take place?"

At the entrance to the port, an orchestra and a troupe of dancers awaited the solemn moment. The mayor of Choshi was present; he handed me a good luck banner, the central motif of which was a fish, and gave a short speech, which he then translated into perfect French. An admirer from Saudi Arabia, who had taken his vacation to be here expressly for the occasion, gave me a copy of the Koran. Though I didn't read or speak a word of Arabic, he assured me it would stand me in good stead because of the volume's "great symbolic virtues." *Allah Akbar!*

The most original gift was that given by the president of the Choshi Yacht Club (which consisted, as far as I could make out, of three stout craft). It was a telephone calling card, which I was to keep with me throughout my trip and guard with my life. When I arrived in America, I was to present it with his compliments to his opposite number in the United States, which, I presumed, meant the president of the yacht club of whatever American port I put in to.

In short, it was a festivity fully worthy of the occasion, with the one exception that the occasion being celebrated would unfortunately not be taking place.

How could I explain to that august gathering that both my instruments of communication, usually so dependable, were for all intents and purposes worthless, and that without them there was no way I could put out to sea?

The manufacturer of the nonfunctioning telex was French, which presented an immediate problem because of the time difference between France and Japan. We had to place our calls at night, knowing that we would never find anyone in the Paris office outside working hours. Our various efforts to make contact were highly comical, except none of us was laughing. While I tried to get through by telex from the boat, Christopher would dash off to a phone booth a kilometer away and place a call through the international operator. When he finally did get through, the manufacturer invariably declared that he had not received any telex, would then suggest trying another procedure, et cetera. Christopher would then return to the boat, attempt to implement the suggestion, try to transmit again, then dash back to the phone booth. Several nights were spent in this vain endeavor.

We also had a few fun moments with the radio. The French importer from whom we had bought the equipment had of his own volition suggested a number of technical improvements that could enhance the instrument's capabilities — modifications that in my estimation were indispensable. When all our efforts in Choshi to make the radio function properly failed, we called the importer in France. His answers were evasive. Then he had a revelation: the radio was of Japanese origin, so to make it work, or at least find out what was wrong with it, all we had to do was contact the local representative of the company. Simple as shooting fish in a barrel!

Seeing a ray of hope on the horizon, we got in contact with the local technician. Once we explained the nature of the problem, he acted as though he had just been struck with some form of local paralysis. The risk was just too great. The very notion that he might be held responsible for our project's failure was more than he could bear. He bowed respectfully before the problem and vanished into the night.

We now had no choice but to take the instrument to Tokyo, to the headquarters of the company that had made it. A careful preoperative examination revealed that the original product had been modified after it had left the factory. Bad omen. The Japanese engineer put in a call to the French importer. Had modifications been made on the instrument?

This gave our French colleague a readymade out. "If the radio isn't working, it's probably because of the modifications made specifically at Monsieur d'Aboville's request. I should add that we strongly advised him against making those modifications."

That was all the Japanese manufacturer needed to hear. Relieving the radio of all its carefully structured modifications, he returned it to us in its pristine state. The only problem was, in its pristine state the radio still didn't work.

Christopher was beside himself. In despair, he telephoned an expert someone had touted to him, a certain Mr. Takedo, with whom he made an appointment for that same afternoon. Punctual to a fault, Christopher showed up at Mr. Takedo's workplace only to find that he, too, had mysteriously disappeared. Subsequently, in talking to one of our suppliers, we learned what had happened: apparently, the main office had called all its retailers and ordered them not to make any effort to repair the mad Frenchman's radio. Poor Mr. Takedo, overwhelmed with remorse at the idea that he would not be able to honor our appointment, had preferred to vanish into the woodwork rather than face us with the bad news.

As for our fearless importer back home, his backside well covered, I wondered if he realized that because of him we were working around the clock, that he had immobilized eight of his compatriots by his dereliction of duty, and that my chances of leaving under any reasonably acceptable conditions were practically nil?

June 26

As I emerged from the Riverside Hotel in the morning, I had an unexpected and totally pleasant surprise: my cousin François was standing there to greet me.

François, looking for all the world like a gentleman

farmer — and more gentleman than farmer in this instance — was almost like a brother to me. I say "almost" because I already have five brothers and adding one more might have been more than the family could bear. I was delighted to see him: his mere presence gave my morale a much-needed boost. Together with the faithful and indefatigable Bruno and Christopher, he was part of the hardcore group of old friends who I knew could help combat the case of demoralization that was already threatening to decimate our ranks.

Hastily sworn in as our de facto chief of protocol, François departed posthaste on a diplomatic mission to the French embassy in Tokyo. There he had the good fortune to meet the military attache, Commander Blanvillain, to whom he related the sad story of our radio and telex.

Blanvillain was not only aware of our project but a staunch supporter; he told François he would do everything in his power to help. True to his word, the next day he dispatched an embassy communications specialist, Georges de Marrez, to examine our equipment and see if he could come up with a solution. The minute he arrived, he went to work on the recalcitrant telex machine. Watching de Marrez work was inspirational. If I told you he was stubborn — no, tenacious — take my word for it. We tried everything. We took the whole thing apart, piece by piece, and put it back together again. I even went so far as to move the boat to different points in the Choshi port, to counteract a hypothetical electrical line or antenna that might be interfering with our transmission.

Yet afternoon merged into evening, evening into night, and still no success. By morning, I had made up my mind: either we would find another telex or I would leave without one.

*　　*　　*

With each passing day, I was exchanging one day of summer navigation for an extra day of winter navigation that I would have to endure at the end of the crossing. When the incessant rain finally let up a bit, giving me hope that the better weather might hold up for several days, I made up my mind to leave in two days' time, that is, on June 30.

June 30

This morning, the final straw. And sickening to boot. The strong easterly winds had blown an awful conglomeration of filth and garbage into the boat basin: every sort of debris imaginable — countless dead fish, bits and pieces of fishing nets, plastic bags — all held together by a thick layer of greasy, fetid foam. The choppy waves in the port had borne the stinking mass into the inner basin and coated *Sector*'s hull, which was unrecognizable. The cockpit had become unusable, as had the mooring lines. In fact, everything we touched immediately became polluted. Even the ladder from the dock down into the boat was covered with the awful slime.

I sat down on the dock beside Bruno, who had slept on board the previous night, and contemplated the disaster. We looked up to discover that our camera crew, alert to any new situation, was assiduously shooting the scene. Poor Laurent, our director: I, who have a hard time under ordinary conditions keeping myself upbeat in front of the camera, had to be the worst of subjects now. All I could come up with, in a weak show of black humor, was: "It's a shame you can't film the smell."

For, in addition to the greasy substance itself, the harbor

was filled with a sewerlike stench that impregnated our clothes, our hair, even our skin.

And yet, we had to get on with it. Georges had managed to repair the radio, which seemed to be working fine. As for the telex, the hell with it! We lifted *Sector* out of the water in order to rid it of its stinking outer growth. Its hull had earlier been treated with an antifouling paint to keep marine vegetation from attaching itself and growing there, which would have slowed my progress. The delicate problem was that to remove the foul matter we had to scrub, and scrub hard, but in doing so we had to be careful not to scrape off the antifouling paint. As for the gear, we cleaned it by resorting to the products normally reserved for scrubbing toilets; nothing less seemed to have an effect.

To top this, a swarm of Japanese photographers had descended on Choshi that morning, which had been announced — once again — as the real departure day. They were kept at a distance by a rope cordon we had set up about thirty feet from the boat. Intent on immortalizing the departure of the mad rower from their shores, they were more than a trifle puzzled by the stem-to-stern scouring that was taking place before them. I thought the scene was self-explanatory, but apparently it was not, and finally I had to go explain to them — trying to keep my frayed temper in check — exactly what had happened. I kept thinking, I've been so insanely busy — to no good end, I might add — that I haven't even had time to make contact with my family, and here I am explaining the obvious to a group of journalists I don't give a damn about.

By the end of that trying day, my hands were red and raw from the harsh cleaning products we had used. Not an ideal situation for one who is supposed to start rowing tomorrow.

During the night, about one o'clock in the morning to be exact, I had a sudden revelation: I realized that I was giving in to an insane desire to leave, to flee. What I was fleeing from, however, was basically my irritation at this interminable waiting period. No, that wasn't the only reason. Every evening, as the days went by, I pictured myself confronting that increasingly insurmountable obstacle: the October and November storms that I knew were waiting for me on the other side of the ocean.

I also knew I was worn out; I was not thinking clearly. The weather was still unstable at best. The slight improvement we had just seen was predicted not to last, at least not long enough for me to leave under reasonable, if not optimum, conditions. Chances were, if I left now, the first strong easterly winds that came up would drive me right back onto the Japanese mainland.

About two in the morning, in a state of panic, I woke up Christopher.

"Christopher, do you realize my 'last interview before the departure,' that we gave to the television people, is just arriving in Paris? We can't let it be shown —

"Hold everything, Christopher. I have to think things out. . . . But I know one thing — I'm not leaving tomorrow."

July 5

I was wiped out. For almost three weeks now we had been struggling to get the boat ready, and I was in a state of total exhaustion.

Telex still not working, endless formalities, lousy weather. . . . Every day, more often than not twice a day,

39

Mitsuru accompanied me to the weather bureau for the latest updates. For the past two weeks one low pressure system after another had moved in, interspersed with violent storms and varying winds.

When I asked the weatherman what he thought the next few days would bring, he smiled and shook his head in a manner that he assumed would be as uncompromising as possible. Again, the constant concern about not making a mistake, but it should be noted that in Japan one's professional integrity and sense of honor are virtually limitless. One of my Japanese friends, the director of Mobil Oil Japan, in whom I confided the problems I was having trying to get some accurate forecasts, told me a story. A few years ago, some weathermen had announced the arrival of the rainy season, a rather important date in the Japanese calendar. The appointed day came and went without a drop of rain. Ditto the next day, and the day after. In fact, a whole week went by without any sign of rain, at which point two of the meteorologists committed suicide.

The daily countdown to departure day had ceased. I had the feeling the whole endeavor had gone down the drain. All this time and energy wasted — for nothing!

By now we had become part of the landscape at the Choshi boat basin in which poor *Sector* was ensnared. On the dock, a makeshift tent sheltered our equipment from the endless rain. A few visitors continued to show up every day, waiting for their daily briefing. Bruno politely tried to update them, in a mixture of French and English, about the basics of the boat or the trip itself. Which gave birth to something like this:

"Well, you see, this boat, given its length and its lack of

ballast, can obviously capsize. So, when that happens, there is this ingenious system of ballast . . ."

The heads would nod in unison.

". . . so, *Sector* is outfitted with reservoirs, each of which contains a hundred liters, one to starboard, the other to port. Now then, thanks to this little hand pump, Gerard, who is stationed inside his watertight cabin when the boat has turned over, can fill one or another of these lateral ballast tanks with sea water to throw the boat off balance, as it were, which, in conjunction with the movement of the waves, enables it to right itself. Do you understand?"

The heads would nod in unison.

Emboldened by this show of interest, Bruno would continue: "A third ballast tank, situated at the stern of the boat, enables you to control the trim, is that clear? . . ."

By now the crowd would have grown, its attention riveted on Bruno's every word; despite the continued collective motion of the group's heads there was no assurance anything had gotten through. Nonetheless, Bruno would forge on, as though he were addressing the graduating class of the naval institute.

"This weight in the stern, together with the two antidrift plates that can be lowered whenever one wants, serve the purpose of keeping the stern facing into the waves in foul weather. . . . Pretty clever, no?"

The heads would nod in unison.

Bruno had become an important fixture in the Choshi boat basin. His many admirers, concerned about his well-being, furtively left sandwiches or mineral water for us on several occasions.

How Bruno operated with complete success whenever he went into town to run one errand or another, we never knew. What we did know was that he had the neighborhood

41

in his back pocket. Among his conquests was the local hardware store owner, from whom Bruno could get whatever we needed or wanted. It was at the hardware store that Bruno met Mrs. Takasse, a French woman married to a Japanese from Choshi. Both Mr. and Mrs. Takasse showered us with countless bounties during that trying period, for which we'll never forget them. We liked the couple immediately: for one thing, they were the only couple in town who drove a beat-up old car without dying of shame.

During this period, my growing reputation as the French equivalent of a kamikaze — those who set off knowing they were going to certain death — greatly enhanced my reputation with the municipal officials and, in more than one instance, ended up putting me in situations that I can only describe as surreal.

"Do you like oysters?" the honorable mayor, our host, asked me through the interpreter.

I was having trouble concentrating on the question because I was still trying to figure out how to sit properly at this low-slung Japanese table. That is, how could I cross my overly long legs in such a way that I could approach the table without my knees looming high above it, thus preventing any possible access to it or the food?

Oysters. The word finally penetrated, and a vague feeling of unease overwhelmed me, the still wary foreigner, as I parried one question with another.

"How do you eat them here in Japan?" I asked the interpreter.

The question was duly relayed to the mayor, who smiled — smugly, I thought — and responded, "Raw, of course. And on the half-shell. Not like the Americans with their oysters Rockefeller!"

Slightly reassured, I was able to turn my attention once

again to my left leg, which was at this point fast asleep.

Christopher had been watching me wrestle with my legs and could not keep from laughing out loud. He had solved the leg problem by kneeling in front of the table. I decided I would wait till the last dinner course before taking my revenge. I would point out to him that, even though I was suffering physically from crossing my legs Japanese style, I felt it my duty to remind him that his kneeling position was one assumed only by women in Japan, which meant that throughout the evening he, suave, macho Christopher, had served as a constant source of amusement for our honorable hosts. My Machiavellian mind had already formed a picture of his pained contortions upon hearing this bit of local custom, as he frantically tried to work his legs into the proper position.

Meanwhile, I was still struggling with my own lower limbs. I had indeed gotten my left leg crossed under my right, but the aforementioned problem of soaring knees, forming a double Mount Fuji between me and the table, had still not been solved. I glanced discreetly at my Japanese colleagues. How in the world did they manage?

These biotechnical problems, however, were interrupted by the untimely arrival of the oysters. They say that for those on their way to the guillotine, all minor aches and pains magically disappear. Mine did when I saw the size of the bivalves. I had never seen anything remotely like them. Monsters is the only word that came to mind. And, it goes without saying, the mayor had honored me by serving me the largest of the lot, the oyster queen, which must have weighed a good five pounds. That's right: *five* pounds. If there had been a bivalve book of records, this one would have deserved at least a full paragraph. Its shell would have made a lovely wash basin or perfect baptismal font. All I could think of when I saw it was that it had to be the expectoration of some giant creature of the ocean depths.

This was no oyster! Whatever it was, it was served on the proverbial silver platter.

I played for time.

"And pray tell, your honor, where did you find such a beauty?"

"Right here, just outside the port."

All I could think of was the thousands of gallons of sewage-laden water the creature had filtered through its giant, grayish self.

I glanced over at Christopher, seated opposite me, and it was as though I were looking in a mirror. He was green — which, I was sure, was my color as well — his eyes popping as he gazed in a combination of awe and terror at his own beast. His forehead was bathed in sweat, and his Adam's apple bobbed up and down uncontrollably.

I shifted my position so as not to be directly across from him.

Warily my eyes searched around the room for some po-tential dumping ground. The only vague hope was a flower pot, but it was a good ten feet away. Would I have time to plant another flower in the pot? I needed some diversionary tactic but could think of none.

Meanwhile, my Japanese colleagues, having noisily in-gurgitated their respective delicacies, as if to show us how it was done, were politely waiting for us to follow their good example.

In total desperation, Christopher tried to pull a fast one: he picked up the shell with both hands, brought it to his mouth, made a loud sucking noise without so much as touching the oyster itself, then put the oyster back on the table and quickly closed the shell. Then he groped for the top of the serving platter to quickly conceal his sin.

Well done, Christopher! And he would doubtless have gotten away with it, if a discreet but ultra-efficient waiter had not removed the cover of the serving platter just as

Christopher took the oyster away from his mouth. I noted that Christopher's eyes resembled those of a wild horse at the very idea that his lips had come in close contact with the creature.

To cover his embarrassment, he quickly poured himself a cup of tea.

All right, let's get it over with. Deep inspiration. I stared at the enemy, Medusa in the depths of her pool. Clearly she knows — she stares back at me just as fixedly. If I were not mistaken, I thought I detected a tiny tremor. Who is going to swallow whom? I teased her with my chopsticks, as a way of getting to know her a trifle better. I concocted a battle plan, whereby I would attack the flanks, which might give me at least a fighting chance of ignoring the grayish-white critical mass that occupied the center of the swamp. The moment of truth: the edge of the shell was raised to my mouth, my eyes were closed, my throat constricted, my temples moist. . . . There it goes, on its way, let 'er rip! My mouth was full of oyster, yet I had a sinking feeling that more than half of it was still in the shell.

Several ideas raced through my mind. Return the first half to its shell? Bite down hard on it and swallow the first half? The very idea of having to start the operation all over again dissuaded me from either course, and I did my best to relax my throat muscles. The reconnaissance patrol of the monster was already wallowing in my stomach while the rear guard was still languishing in the shell. I was suffocating, but I had no choice but to push on. There was certainly no going back!

Finally, like a cormorant swallowing a fish whole, I felt first my mouth, then my throat, slowly — very slowly — revert to its normal state. My stomach reacted with a series of violent spasms. I gulped down some hot tea, which burned me terribly but comforted me with the knowledge that I was also scalding the beast below, which, I was sure,

45

was busily exploring its new domain. I felt one last spasm . . . then quiet. It was over.

Christopher looked at me in disbelief. I returned to this world with the comforting thought that I would now have the rare pleasure of watching Christopher perform the same ceremony.

"Would you care for another?" the mayor asked solicitously through the mouth of the interpreter, who added, with more than a touch of malice, "It's the custom here."

I had a vision of the gigantic internal copulation that would doubtless take place in the event that, were I to follow local custom and down a second, one turned out to be male and the other female. The idea was more than I could bear. I did my best to minimize the potential insult my refusal might provoke by replying, in a tone that brooked no further comment, pitting local custom against local custom:

"Thank you very much, your honor. But you see, in France we *never* eat two oysters on the same day!"

On the weather front, the days followed one another in dreary succession. A warm, steady rain fell endlessly on Choshi. The expedition sank slowly into a state of total torpor. Actually not total: it was divided into two camps. One group was up to its ears in work; the other had absolutely nothing to do. Christopher, François, and Bruno were constantly occupied on all fronts, both technical and administrative. The first two spent much of their time, and all their patience and psychic energy, in the offices and stores of Tokyo, doing battle to make sure all our needs, material and bureaucratic, were taken care of. Bruno, on the other hand, continued to administer to the slightest needs of *Sector* as if it were his only child. As for the others, once the novelty of the situation had worn off and the shopping possibilities in Choshi were exhausted — which, given the size and nature of the town, did not take long — their patience was growing thinner by the minute.

The date of my departure seemed more problematic with every passing day, and I suggested to several people who had come out to cover the event that they ought to fly home. My well-meant suggestion was greeted with a great hue and cry of protest. Having come all this way, there was no way they were going to leave until they had seen, and duly recorded on film, my actual departure. I yielded to their vehement objections, only to find a few days later that they had completely reversed themselves and felt they must leave immediately. The endless drizzle, the depressing site, and the unbearable wait had broken their spirit.

Unfortunately, Laurent was obliged to go back with them. He had come out for eight days, and he had already been here a full three weeks. He was due to get married in two days.

From time to time I had myself driven to the lighthouse, situated on top of the cliff that dominated the port, to pose for publicity pictures. There we would exchange pleasantries as I would gesture grandly out to sea, toward America . . . but my heart was no longer in it. We joked and laughed, which was meant to keep our minds off our problems, but deep down I was riddled with doubt.

The wisest thing would be to put off the crossing until next year. The only problem was that I felt like a diver who has been standing too long on the edge of the high-diving board: the longer I stayed the less I wanted to climb down the ladder. Or, to push the analogy further, I felt like the diver who keeps moving to higher and higher boards, upping the risk each time he does.

I never alluded to the idea that we might postpone the trip. I knew if I did, it would get me thinking that it was a real possibility. Instead, my mind was still obsessed only with the idea of departure. Without realizing it, I now understood that I had been pumping myself up, day after day; without that constant self-motivation, there was no way I could bring the project to fruition. For months, even though I was clearly and constantly aware of how hard the crossing would be, all I could think of was the final goal: my arrival at the other end, somewhere on the West Coast of the United States. For months, I had no longer really been of this world: my every thought, my every act, had been focused on that objective. There was no way out. It was not as if I were simply in the starting blocks. It was as if the race were already underway.

To be sure, if my main goal had been to make sure I would end up in some prominent position in the record books, it would have made perfect sense to postpone the trip and leave under better conditions. But I didn't give a damn whether my exploit ended up in the *Guiness Book of Records*, sandwiched somewhere between the smallest man on earth and the champion hotdog-eater. My only public was myself. I was my own sole spectator and judge, for the simple reason that I was the only one who could appreciate the full price of victory.

In posing this challenge to myself, I had set out to reach a goal that I imagined was just barely possible, perhaps even beyond my own presumed limits. Why, then, should I turn my back on these profound self-imposed motivations by postponing the trip till next year on the grounds that it would be easier then and that no one but me would know the difference?

Day after day I kept pushing back my absolutely final departure day, well beyond the earlier "final" dates I had set. I couldn't help remembering that virtually all of those earlier "final" dates had, as they came and went, struck me as dangerously late.

July 10

The sky seemed to be clearing, the weather predictions were right on the money, and to top things off, Georges had installed a brand new telex, which appeared to be working fine. It was as if I had just been handed my exit visa.

During the afternoon, Mitsuru drove me one last time to Cape Inubosaki, from which we had an excellent view to the east. The sea was calm, the winds had fallen. For a long time I gazed out to sea, where a number of ships seemed fixed on the horizon. A visit to the weather bureau confirmed that the bad weather was moving off to northern Japan. No storms were expected for the next several days. Once again, I filled out the forms officially permitting me to leave the country.

On our way back to the boat basin, I had asked Mitsuru to stop at the local barber shop. There I got a shave and a haircut. It was a symbolic gesture; before I go into combat, I need to feel that I look my best.

The barber, who recognized me, refused to accept any money. In exchange, he asked me to give him two autographs. Mitsuru calculated that at the going rate for a shave and haircut, each signature was worth 500 yen, about four dollars, and wondered aloud how much one might be worth a few months from now.

For my last night on land, I repaired to a small wooden house that the Takasses had placed at my disposal. For company I had a hardy troupe of mosquitoes and a shot of whisky. My baggage was all packed: the bag of clothes, forever impregnated with the stench of the befouled boat basin, was packed and ready for shipment back to France; my own bag, much smaller, was also zipped up and ready to be stowed on board.

Until one in the morning I wrote a number of brief letters and postcards. I found it hard to put into words what I was feeling. Then I put in a call to Cornélia. I tried to be as reassuring as possible, telling her that the good weather had finally returned, that the boat was shipshape, that the new telex had been installed and was working fine, that I would be in contact with her frequently. But she was not taken in by this. How could I lessen the impact of that brief but overwhelming phrase, "I'm leaving tomorrow"?

That calm and solitary night in the Takasses' dollhouse reminded me of what soldiers must have felt the night before going into battle. I was fully aware of the formidable ordeal that lay ahead. I was not simply setting out to sea; I was setting forth to battle. And the enemy was the ocean itself. In the surrounding darkness, I felt as though I were recharging my batteries, refocusing my energy and attention on the upcoming combat. I knew how tough a fight it would be, and I needed to be alone tonight, to concentrate and prepare for it. My friends had felt that as well, and I knew that, as I lay here by myself awaiting sleep, they were bedded down beside the *Sector*, each lost in his own thoughts.

A night, too, to grapple with my own solitude, and make it mine. Before it seized me in its own invincible grip.

3

Ahead of Me,
an Enormous Void . . .

July 11

0500: The automobile — with Christopher at the wheel
(driving, I should add, with uncharacteristic restraint) —
pulled up at the dock next to *Sector*. On the way, we had
barely exchanged two words.

"It reminds me of the first day of school. . . ."

"That's true. The first day of boarding school."

A number of people were waiting for me on the dock,
about thirty in all, among them Commander Blanvillain
and several other Frenchmen who had come up from Tokyo
to witness the departure. Thankfully, there were few
photographers or cameramen in sight.

And, of course, there was Bruno, bless his heart, who
had spent the previous night cleaning the hull one last time.
The boat was spick-and-span. On the radio antenna waved
the French flag and, following custom, the Rising Sun.

Everyone seemed to be more or less holding their emotions in check, but there was an almost palpable tension,
which I preferred to cut short.

"Excuse me, gentlemen, but I have many miles to travel
before the sun goes down. . . ."

Before setting off, I had both Christopher and Bruno sign
the first page of my log. My intent was to have them both

sign the last page on the other side of the ocean, if all went well. Despite all our efforts at self-control, I couldn't help noticing more than a few moist eyes. And we seemed to be beyond words; our glances were eloquent enough.

Oars at the ready. A wave of my hand, a smile I meant to be reassuring, and off I set, at a steady stroke. . . . I stared straight into space, to make sure I didn't see any expressions on the faces of those I was leaving behind, then guided the craft out beyond the boat basin into the gentle waters of the Tone River. The ebb tide bore me swiftly toward the river's mouth. And yet, even with all the help I was getting from the current, with each stroke of the oars I kept thinking, "Good God, this thing is heavy, really heavy — and to think I'm going to have to row it clear across this whole damned ocean!"

After I crossed the last breakwater, I lowered the antenna and removed the flags. *Sector* was assuming its sailing trim.

My friends had boarded a fishing boat and were following me at a discreet distance, knowing that I was already alone. At 1700 hours their boat came abreast the *Sector,* then stopped. I gazed intently at their faces one last time, as if I were filling my memory to the brim, to take with me as much of them as I possibly could, although in my heart of hearts I knew it was an illusion. We waved to each other, but as their boat came about I felt that they, and I, were already far apart.

I passed a few trawlers that were returning to Choshi, but none gave me even the slightest hint of recognition. Word had doubtless not yet reached these local fisherman of the exploit of the mad *gai jin* (foreigner).

The *Condor,* a sailboat, which like all those that sailed these waters was more than a trifle squalid, had joined me at the river's mouth. Captain Yagi, the skipper of the *Condor,* had been a stalwart friend and helper throughout my stay in Choshi, and he had invited Mitsuru on board to escort me a dozen or so miles out to sea. One final glance from boat to boat, one final farewell. . . . At long last, the moment of truth had arrived. Strangely, I felt relieved.

The helmsmen of a sailboat who sets out to sea has a tendency to detach himself quickly from his earthbound past. Heading toward the open sea, his mind is already on the distant shores far beyond the horizon toward which he is sailing. Whereas I, a poor rower facing backward, had to measure with each stroke of the oars the pitiful progress I had made — not in nautical miles but only in feet or, at most, yards! But on the day I left, the fog, just as it had done eleven years ago off Cape Cod, came to my assistance; it moved in and cut off any sight of land.

I finally had time to think. I suddenly realized how much I had lived over the past several weeks on nervous energy alone, how much I had acted from day to day simply in response to the constant demands: I had been like an arrow streaking toward its target. I thought of my family, from whom I had now been separated for five weeks. I thought of the phone call I had made the night before to Cornélia. And I thought of Guillaume and Ann as well, and then, as I rowed, I had the odd thought that I was actually moving farther and farther away from them with each stroke of the oars, for the simple reason that Choshi was closer to France than my present position. In fact, it would not be until I had crossed the international dateline, almost in the middle

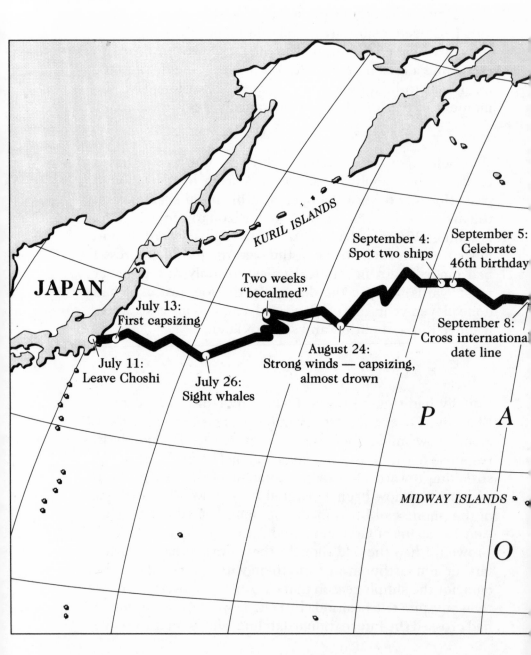

JAPAN

KURIL ISLANDS

July 13:
First capsizing

Two weeks
"becalmed"

September 4:
Spot two ships

September 5:
Celebrate
46th birthday

July 11:
Leave Choshi

July 26:
Sight whales

August 24:
Strong winds — capsizing,
almost drown

September 8:
Cross international
date line

P A

MIDWAY ISLANDS

O

54

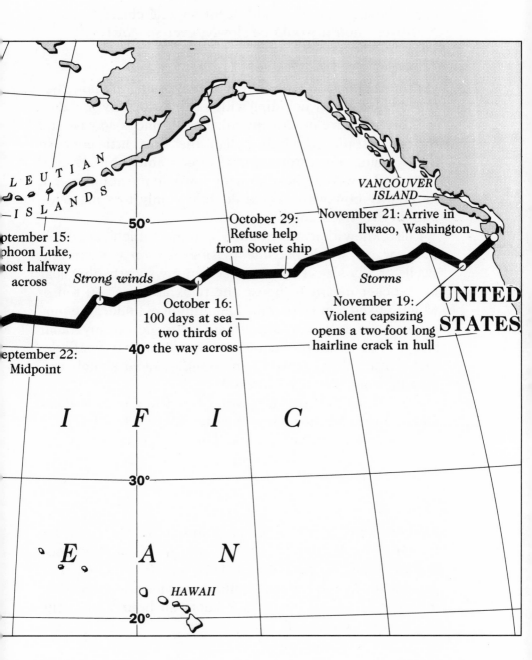

September 15:
Typhoon Luke,
almost halfway
across

Strong winds

September 22:
Midpoint

October 16:
100 days at sea —
two thirds of
the way across

50°

40°

October 29:
Refuse help
from Soviet ship

LEUTIAN
ISLANDS

VANCOUVER
ISLAND

November 21: Arrive in
Ilwaco, Washington

Storms

November 19:
Violent capsizing
opens a two-foot long
hairline crack in hull

UNITED
STATES

I F I C

30°

E A N

HAWAII

20°

of my voyage, that I would begin moving closer to them. And even then it would be slowly, ever so slowly. . . .

On the far horizon a few ships were crossing my bow. But the chances of my colliding with a cargo ship anytime during the trip were practically nil. The Pacific is so vast and the ocean traffic so relatively light that I had little concern that I might encounter a tanker or container ship. Even if I did, and it were to bear straight down on me at full speed, its mighty bow wave would doubtless only toss me aside like an oversized cork.

I also knew that a boat such as mine, which sat so low in the water, would become invisible as soon as it ran into swells of any size. I therefore set up my spearfishing gear in a socket meant to house the telex antenna, on top of which I fixed a honeycombed aluminum cylinder, the purpose of which was to accentuate my echo on any radar screen. I also had on board a minireceiver that would detect, for a radius of two or three miles, radar signals emanating from any nearby vessel.

Nonetheless, during the several days when I was still not far from the shipping lanes of eastern Japan, I had to keep a close lookout for vessels that were not picked up by my receiver. As I would have to do once I reached the coastal waters of the United States.

For the moment, I was keeping an eye on the speed log built into the dashboard, which kept track of both my speed and the nautical miles rowed. I was maintaining a steady pace of seventeen strokes a minute, which was propelling me forward at the rate of 1.8 knots an hour. About the speed of someone walking.

I took a break for lunch. Then I made the first entry in my canvas-covered logbook, which would be the public record of this trip:

1330: Alone at last. Quite moved. I'm trying to picture what Christopher and Bruno are up to. Thoughts that still link me with the world of the living, which will soon blur and disappear. Ahead of me, an enormous void . . .

Evening. An unhappy surprise. Just after having covered my first fifteen nautical miles — a pretty good day — the wind veered from northeast to east. The weather report had promised the opposite. The problem was, if the wind rose, and kept up, it could easily push me back to my point of departure. A humiliating thought.

I'd been rowing for twelve hours, and the predeparture tensions still weighed heavily on me. Given the cumulative fatigue of the past few weeks, it was essential that I get some rest. I set out my big sea anchor, a plastic-covered canvas cone just under three feet in diameter, whose job it was to keep me from drifting backward.

Lying on my bunk in the watertight cabin, I felt as if I were inside some infernal machine whose goal it was to knock me out. For what was happening was that each time a wave came by and lifted the boat, the anchor rope would grow taut and the boat would be yanked backward. Then, when the boat dropped into the wave's trough, its hull would slam down on the surface of the water, taking a terrible beating. The only comparison I can think of out of my own experience was being perched on top of a truck rumbling down a bumpy, rutted road somewhere in Africa.

Needless to say, it was impossible to sleep.

*   *   *

No boat is perfect. It's always a five-footed beast, and this was especially true of mine. It had to be both light and solid, capable of performing in good weather and foul, narrow-beamed and low enough in the water to facilitate rowing, without ballast yet conceived in such a way that it could right itself in the event it capsized. It required in the stern a watertight cabin to house me and in the bow an area, also watertight, large enough to stock six months' worth of provisions. All that without turning into a maritime monster that would be impossible to maneuver.

The conception of an oceangoing rowboat represents, to my mind, despite its deceptive simplicity, a minor miracle of nautical engineering.

What I would have loved to have done was to conceive of, then build, the *Sector* from the first sketch to the final piece of equipment — which is what I did for the *Captain Cook*. But the time frame was against me, so I was obliged to call upon a naval architect, Jean Barret. The advantage of an architect over an artisan like myself is the computer. Every single measurement of the model used to create the mold of the boat is entered onto a computer program. In turn, the builder is supplied with a laser printout based on that model, which enables him to form, rapidly and with great precision, the actual hull and deck.

When I received the plans for *Sector,* I was surprised to see that the bottom of the boat was quite flat. My good old *Captain Cook* had been constructed with a classic, V-shaped hull, similar to the whaling boats of the nineteenth century, which, as far as I was concerned, were as close to perfect as a rowboat can get. Maybe I'm just too much of a traditionalist. Today's naval architects are obviously used to designing light sailboats for the purpose of attaining high speeds, which justifies their flat bottoms. Nonetheless, in my case I remained skeptical.

The knocking about I suffered that night only tended to confirm my intuition: the farther I progressed in my crossing, the more I saw that the flat bottom is not only a source of discomfort, it also slows the progress of the boat each time the sea is rough; instead of slicing through the waves, the prow is lifted by the wave, then slapped back down into the water.

For the moment, however, all that was idle speculation. *Sector* was what it was, and would have to suffice till I got to the other side.

July 12

Up at 0330 hours. An inauspicious start for my second day at sea: the damned easterly wind was still blowing, and the waves were so choppy that I had to row full tilt just to inch ahead a ridiculous few feet. Before long I noticed that even that slight forward progress had slowed to a standstill. Forced to fall back on my wits, I anchored to a fishing buoy I happened to spot along my route. That windfall, however, turned out to be short-lived; a few hours later a fishing boat came by to pick up its catch, leaving me, the parasite, high and dry.

At nightfall, I shifted the sea anchor to the stern post, so that I would be less battered by the waves. Yet my second night at sea was incredibly rough. The east wind intensified:

there were a series of violent storms, with lightning and torrential rain. I remained locked tight in my cabin, preferring to run the risk of snapping the sea anchor rather than drift back toward shore.

At first light, another unpleasant surprise: I could see the coast, less than five miles away! So close that I could clearly see the headlights of cars. I hauled in the sea anchor and started rowing, but at best I was staying put, merely compensating for the easterly drift. Sooner or later, I knew, I would run out of gas and be forced back on shore.

As it grew lighter, the shoreline loomed large and near, and I gazed at it in cold fury, as though it were my mortal enemy. My hands locked on the oars. . . . I had the feeling that the swells were getting bigger here, a sure sign that I was in coastal waters. I began to row like one possessed, furious at the notion that this voyage might shortly come to an ignominious end. I cursed myself for having slept for several hours, but without that precious rest how would I have survived?

And then, at about 1000 hours, the heavens took pity on me: there was a break in the clouds, and the winds abated as quickly as they had come up. Little by little the shoreline receded and at length disappeared into the fog. Late in the afternoon, the sounding line placed beneath the hull informed me that the water temperature was rising very rapidly. Between 1500 and 1900 hours, it rose from 18 to 25 degrees centigrade (about 64 to 77 degrees Fahrenheit). That, I knew, was a most propitious sign, because it meant I had picked up the Kuroshio, the warm current that originates in the southern part of the Japanese archipelago and dissipates in the colder waters of the northern Pacific. It is the Asian equivalent of the Gulf Stream, which had played its part in helping me across the Atlantic a decade earlier. Contrary to popular belief, these two warm streams are not like two broad rectilinear boulevards but rather resemble two huge snakes that undulate across hundreds of ocean miles. The Kuroshio, at the spot where I was navigating, flows from the southwest to the northeast at about three knots an hour, which is extremely fast for an ocean current. I knew that I would only have its blessed "tailwaters" for ten days or so, but while I was with it I wanted to use it to the best of my ability: it literally quadrupled my daily speed. Because of its meandering course, however, on several occasions I rowed beyond its uncertain boundaries and had to pick it up again to benefit a bit longer from its beneficent flow.

That evening, the weather grew cooler and the winds shifted to the north, virtually 180 degrees from the direction of the current. This kind of situation gives rise to rough and very unpredictable seas. It also gave rise to a spectacular show that I can describe only as unreal: as the waves broke against each other, their crests shone with an incandescent brightness. The ocean, as though electrified, was putting on a fantastic show of nautical fireworks. What was causing the phenomenon were millions of tiny living organisms that filled the waters and, like marine fireflies, made them luminescent.

I put out the sea anchor, to stabilize the boat and make sure it was heading in the right direction, and let it run with the tide. I retired to my cabin, pleased with the thought that throughout the night I would be making northeasterly progress. No sooner had I stretched out on the bunk, however, than the old routine, dating back to my voyage on the *Captain Cook*, resurfaced. Golden rules, to be always and utterly followed. Basic rule: never bunk down for the night without having checked the deck and the bow posts to make sure that everything is shipshape in case the boat should capsize during the night. Are the two pairs of oars that are stowed inside, in the cockpit, properly fastened, as well as the pair on deck? Are the sea chests in the cockpit all closed tight?

I had checked and double-checked everything a dozen times before coming aft into the cabin, but still I was plagued by a nagging doubt. I got dressed and went back out to check everything again. The nets that held my provisions in place were all correctly fastened, but I made them even more taut.

I did not like the looks of the sea. In the event the boat did capsize, any shifting of the foodstuffs could make it impossible to right the boat according to plan. To make the craft lighter, *Sector* was constructed without a keel and without any fixed ballast. I knew that there was a good possibility the boat would capsize a number of times in the course of the crossing, so I had provided for that contingency by having a system of ballast tanks built in to remedy the situation. A small manual pump was installed right next to my bunk, which I could use to fill with seawater — or empty — whatever ballast tanks I needed: this would right the boat.

I had to be able to take in seawater through either the hull or the deck when the boat was overturned, because I had to be in a position to transfer weight from one ballast tank to another and simultaneously let air into or out of the tank being emptied or filled. Bruno had spent days on end figuring out this brain-twister and making sure the solution worked. Such a system had to be fitted into a relatively small space, be a hundred percent trustworthy, and be maneuverable with your eyes closed in a capsized boat that has taken on water.

In fact, the sea trials we underwent back in France had left me with mixed feelings on this score. We had used a crane to turn the boat over. I was strapped inside the watertight cabin, in a cramped position that I can only describe as at best uncomfortable, and when I started pumping to shift the ballast in such a way that the boat should have righted itself, nothing happened! For the life of me, I couldn't get the damn thing to turn over. Bruno had to dive in and manually help turn the craft right-side up. When I asked him whether it had been hard for him to do, his reply was only partially reassuring. He said it wasn't easy, but doable. It occurred to me to remind him that out in the Pacific I wouldn't have any Bruno around to dive in and give me a hand, but I refrained.

Still, the experiment had left me pensive. I would obviously have preferred that *Sector* right itself after capsizing, and the shifting ballast method seemed to me less than perfect. I had told myself that my roughly 350 pounds of provisions on board, which would be stowed low on the boat, should help matters. I also rationalized that the sea trial had taken place under the worst conditions possible — that is, in the boat basin where the waters were absolutely calm. If in the course of the crossing the boat did capsize — and I had to assume it would — the movement of the waves would actually help me get it right-side up. I would not, after all, be rowing across some quiet little pond.

As I left the boat at the end of the sea trial, I felt everyone was watching me like a hawk, waiting to see my reaction. I put on my best self-confident smile. But I noted that no one said a word.

Unbearable heat. I retreated into the cabin, leaving the porthole between the cockpit and cabin open to let in a little air. A veritable sauna. Most of the time I lay in the cabin half-stretched out on the short bunk, with my shoulders hunched up to save space, in a crouching position or somewhere in between. Someone seeing me there would think I was practicing to be a contortionist. In the long run, it was exhausting. Not exactly what you would call a gentle little nest, but today the tightness of the living quarters was nothing compared to the withering heat.

I dozed off, knocked out by the tropical heat, but not really able to fall asleep because the boat was jumping about like a bucking bronco. I had the sea anchor out at the stern, and when the waves stretched the anchor rope tight, the stern would slap the water and the whole boat would shake and resonate like an oversize drum.

The open porthole let in a little air but not really enough to cool things off. I was tempted to open the door, but in this weather it was out of the question.

2300: Without warning, the boat suddenly capsized. About 50 liters of water flooded the cabin. A real shambles. All sorts of objects floating. A feeling of fear and distress.

Water poured into the cabin before I had had a chance to close the porthole. I struggled in the darkness and disarray: the cabin was still filled with loose objects that I had not had a chance to stow properly since my departure, including some landlubber clothes I had meant to leave behind, some fresh food I had bought the night before I left, a sleeping bag. All I could think of was that I now knew — locked upside down in the boat — how dirty clothes must feel inside a washing machine.

4

"Rowboat Calling Okera"

So it had happened!

Only two days out and already I had to face the first crucial test of the trip: could I manage to get *Sector* turned right-side up? In total darkness, I steadied myself as best I could, pushed the most irritating floating objects out of my way behind me, and, with my eyes closed, almost automatically began to operate the levers that controlled the ballast. Fifth lever, the one on deck, to the "exhaust" position; third lever, which controlled the starboard reservoir, to the "fill" position; the air exhaust to "open" position — and then I began to pump. A hundred strokes, a hundred-fifty, until the starboard reservoir should have been full. . . .

And now for the moment of truth. I could feel my heart pounding. I felt a wave breaking, shifted all my weight to starboard, and, yes, my little world rotated back into an upright position. *Sector* had passed its first major test with flying colors.

I emptied the ballast, dried the interior of the cabin, and tried to tidy up the precarious microcosm. I had to confess that, though I was fully prepared to cope with the boat's capsizing, I had never expected it would happen so soon. The Pacific had just presented me with its first slap, and I had taken it in stride. So far so good.

*   *   *

This said, the boat was a complete mess, and it would take me hours to make it shipshape. One of the radar housings had taken on water, and I knew I would have to strip the whole thing down, take it apart, and clean it with fresh water. I also had to gather up the various objects and pieces of equipment that had been strewn about and put them back where they belonged. The clothes, too: I stuffed them into a bag, which I stored under the bunk. The ultra-narrow confines of the boat demanded that I keep trying to find better and better means of stowage, so that I would know, immediately and automatically, where everything was at all times, without stopping to think. If nothing else, the previous night's experience had taught me a good lesson.

July 14

It was exactly eleven years ago today that I'd set out to row across the Atlantic. The sea had been calm, the sky clear, and the French tricolor, together with the Stars and Stripes, was smartly displayed on my antenna. That time, too, I had departed later than planned, but the distance to be covered was only half what it was this time. I remembered that on that July 14 — a French national holiday — I celebrated by opening a bottle of Mouton-Rothschild 1978 to toast the day. I also recalled that I had, on that same occasion, experimented with a new technique of novel reading: my book rested on toe clips, and when I got to the end of a page I would turn it with my toes — without missing a stroke of the oars!

Today, in contrast to that earlier holiday, everything was gray. No dolphins sporting, no birds overhead to liven the cheerless seascape. Surrounded by the dark, blue-green waters, I found myself nostalgically hearkening back to the

Gulf Stream, to the deep, sparkling, glossy, almost Mediterranean waters of that other ocean. The beauty of the Atlantic is deeply and inexorably engraved in my mind. Here I was entering a world that was dull, gloomy, and sullen.

July 15

The sky finally cleared, but the wind, still blowing against the current, had kept the sea choppy, so that it was impossible to make any forward progress by rowing alone. The good news was, I was still in the midst of the Kuroshio, which, like Old Man River, just kept rolling along. I was slightly ashamed at making such speed without in any way contributing to it. I only hoped it would keep up.

During the afternoon the sky became overcast, turning a milky white. High clouds. I could tell that a low pressure system was moving in, which buoyed my spirits. That could mean a nice little southwesterly or, even better, a southerly wind, which was exactly what I needed.

Together with strong ocean currents, low pressure systems are a rower's second-best friend when he's looking to pick up a little speed. In contrast to a sailing craft, which can deftly use almost any wind or even waves to its advantage, a rowboat's propulsion is so minimal that it renders one extremely vulnerable. On the other hand, if the wind and water currents are favorable, they not only add to your own efforts but multiply them.

Low pressure systems rotate in a counterclockwise direction. Like water draining from a basin, winds turn and are

67

swallowed up in the center of the low pressure system in order to fill the void. In the Northern Hemisphere, this vortex moves from west to east and inevitably confronted me with the same dilemma: if I caught the top of the spiral I would run into easterly winds that would propel me backward, whereas if I could pick up the bottom of the spiral, I would catch the helpful west winds. Often the two edges of the spiral were no more than a few miles apart, so the whole trick was to avoid the former and find the latter. In fact, the intelligence and finesse of an undertaking such as mine was to make maximum use of both the water currents and the winds.

I was counting on the weather reports out of Japan — which in this early part of my trip I was picking up quite easily — to help me figure where to head to profit from the currents and winds. The problem was, the weather was proving so fickle that it was changing more quickly than I could alter my position. I found myself forever rowing behind the weather reports, which instead of being predictions became postmortems. I had to rely instead on my sense and knowledge of the sea: sniff out the wind, scan the sky and the clouds, and try as best I could — usually by an extra bit of patience or by rowing more hours than usual — to use every atmospheric disturbance to my advantage.

July 16

I let the Kuroshio do most of the work. To row against the strong easterly wind would have obliged me to pull in the sea anchor, and that, no doubt, would have made me move backward even faster. I rowed whenever I felt up to it. The rest of the time I endured.

That night, locked up tight in my cubbyhole, I was swimming in heat and humidity. The sea was getting rougher by the minute. This time I had closed up everything, except for the baffle-plate porthole, an opening so small it didn't even let me see what was going on outside. The only air intake was through one of the sea chests in the cockpit. Curled up in a fetal position on my bunk, I was soaked with sweat. The humidity was such that both the walls and cabin ceiling were streaming with condensed moisture, a real junglelike atmosphere. When I couldn't stand it any longer and decided to open the porthole for a second, I took an unwanted shower.

Sector was being battered unmercifully. Waves were hammering the hull, bouncing the boat about like the proverbial cork, making the whole craft shudder from stem to stern. Each time a wave hit, it shook fat drops of water from the ceiling. But the worst was trying not to listen for the impending crash of a giant wave as it approached the boat. Coming at roughly five-minute intervals, each wave approached with the deafening roar of an express train pounding through a tiny country station. My nerves were stretched to the breaking point, I could see absolutely nothing, and every time I heard a wave coming I steeled myself for the impact. Then, the instant after the wave hit, I felt a staggering blow as it struck the stern, followed by a gigantic left hook to the deck, no more than four inches above my head, which loosed a flood of condensation in the cabin itself. I hardly had time to collect my wits before I heard the next breaker approaching. Instinctively, I pulled my head down into my shoulders and, in utter obscurity, braced myself for the next blow, for the next express train to roar over me in the night.

In the morning, a series of vicious waves swamped the cockpit so quickly that it had no time to empty itself. The cabin itself was inundated, via the baffle-plate porthole, with fifty liters of water.

In the course of the night's battle, I had lost the only stowaway I discovered on board: a mosquito, which had already bitten me several times, but which I had not found the heart to kill.

That cursed machine — the telex — was irritating me more every day. Every evening since my departure I had been trying to hook it up with one of the satellites circling the Pacific and Indian Oceans. Every night I would give up and turn it off. A total fiasco! I thought of all the people who were waiting to hear from me, of all the endless hard work Georges had put in to make sure that this troublesome but absolutely necessary, supposedly sophisticated system of communication worked properly.

As a fallback I resorted to the radio transmitter, which allowed me to use the airwaves reserved for ham operators. These dedicated and ardent "amateurs" are completely respectful of the strict rules and regulations that are intended to protect telephone communications and avoid overloading the airwaves. A number of ham radio operators have banded together in specialized networks whose role it is to cover a large part of the world's oceans, keeping in daily touch with all oceangoing vessels to exchange weather data with them and to be ready, at a moment's notice, to contact the authorities in case a ship runs into serious trouble.

During the evening of July 18 I finally made contact with Okera Net, a network operating out of Japan that covered the western Pacific.

Taking advantage of a lull between two calls, I let out: "Rowboat, calling Okera. Rowboat *Sector,* calling Okera Net."

I could imagine the surprise of the operator on the other end receiving a call from a rowboat! But for a Japanese operator, protocol and procedures are all-important. He asked me to wait my turn: that is, wait until he had finished communicating with the "regulars." I was fit to be tied: six solar panels, set up on the cabin roof and in *Sector's* bow, were my sole source of electricity — a far too precious commodity to be wasted waiting for my turn! Finally I did hook up with him, gave my position, and asked him to transmit it to Christopher, who was still in Japan.

I went to bed delighted by this little exploit. But then I was assailed by a nagging doubt: my English accent is bad, and that of my Japanese contact was, I could tell, even worse. How could I be sure that the information I had given would really get through? I could imagine the consternation of my friends when, the following day, they were informed that I was somewhere in the middle of the Indian Ocean!

July 18

0600: Awake to a sea and sky the color of lead. I pull in the sea anchor to find that it is completely shattered!

Just time to wash up and brush my teeth, then to work sewing the sea anchor back together. To make matters worse, the southwesterly wind had pushed me out beyond

71

the boundaries of the Kuroshio. Damn it all, I had counted on sticking to it for another several days. *Sector* was drifting gently but aimlessly. I decided to climb down into the cockpit and take up the oars, with the goal of rejoining the current on its next leg, which I calculated to be about 120 miles to the east. Besides, I was weary of living this rat's life, lurking in my tiny lair; it was time to shake off the lethargy and get moving.

My progress was uncertain at best, as I had to fight a combination of crosswinds and heavy seas. The dismal sky grew even darker, then it began to rain, and, miracle of miracles, the wind suddenly shifted more than 100 degrees and began to blow in a northwesterly direction. As is so often the case in such a situation, the sea, after a moment's reflection, decided to do whatever it damn well pleased, which was a dozen things at once: waves striking each other at ninety-degree angles, water spouts, steep crests followed by enormous troughs — in short, a sea impossible to judge much less cope with. Yet, thanks to the favorable winds, my little craft had taken wing and was speeding along. The rains had become torrential, but I was absolutely delighted to have rejoined the battle. The rain whipped my face and blinded me; without my sunglasses I couldn't have seen a thing, but with them on I could not only see but they filtered reality and rendered it a shade less gray.

Mechanically, I glanced at the compass. Then over at the speed log. The latter is not an indispensable instrument as far as I am concerned, but it did have the virtue of egging me on, of making me pull harder on the oars. Two and a half knots. . . . I turned to and began stroking at a good, steady pace, determined not to stop until I had recorded a good ten knots.

At the stroke of noon (no pun intended) I had reached

my goal. I checked my position and saw that the current had added another eight nautical miles to my own efforts. Not bad. My morale inched upward.

During lunchbreak I felt a burning sensation on the fleshy part of my anatomy, that part which, even more than your hands, suffers when you row. To have rowed long and hard under a driving rain, without lubrication, had not helped matters either. With the help of an improvised rearview mirror, I managed to examine the area in question, only to discover a disconcerting row of incipient boils — there must have been twenty in all. Small, yellow boils, just waiting to grow up into full-fledged adults, were already forming, one already suppurating. I spread a generous layer of antibiotic jelly over the area. I figured that the movement between buttocks and the rowing seat would take care of massaging it in.

During the afternoon, the sky was still as low as ever, with bolts of lightning at regular intervals and winds that were gusting up to twenty-five miles per hour. But I was moving right along, and by the end of the "working day," I had covered another forty nautical miles. I felt I had a good chance at reaching my goal, that is, catching the top of the next leg of the Kuroshio.

That evening, for the first time, it turned cold. I lighted a candle, whose flame added a bit of warmth to my cabin. But it also generated a condensation of the dampness that permeated the place. My sleeping bag and all my clothes were soaking wet, with a sticky dampness that I couldn't seem to get rid of.

73

July 20

At dawn, I caught sight of two ships, one a trawler, the other a huge cargo ship, heading toward Japan. Before I had finished my coffee, the freighter had disappeared beyond the horizon. I realized that by tomorrow morning it would be tied up at some Japanese port. Today marked my tenth day at sea. Clearly we belonged to different worlds!

I was constantly trying to move farther to the south. Weather reports I received indicated a low pressure system there, which, who knows, could help my progress. I also knew there was a danger in choosing that southerly course. In these latitudes, a mistake in my position could prove costly, for if I guessed wrong I could be sentenced to wander aimlessly to and fro in the middle of the Pacific, caught in some windless high pressure area or slowed down by opposing wind currents.

The sea was less rough, the weather ideal, with a brisk northwest wind of about fifteen to twenty-five knots. I felt there was a good chance for a record-setting day.

Twelve hours of rowing.

Those who have ever rowed crew might well ask how I manage to maintain such a pace day after day. To which I respond that although I keep a steady pace, I never overexert myself; I never row to the point of exhaustion. By racing standards, mine is a heavy boat, with good momentum, and once I get it moving I help the momentum along, I maintain it, but without straining. To make a simple analogy, I am not a runner; I am a walker. But, a walker who has made up his mind to walk, say, from Paris to

Beijing at a pace of fifty kilometers (or roughly thirty miles) a day, no matter how much his feet hurt, no matter what the weather is, through sun and rain, sleet and snow, carrying on his back a knapsack that's a trifle too heavy.

My motor is not so much my muscles, but my stubbornness, my tenacity, my loathing of discouragement, which I have to fight day after day, hour after hour, stroke after stroke, as each arc of the oars grows more difficult than the last. I am a resistance fighter in a war I invented for myself. The enemy is me, with all my physical shortcomings, my temptation to give up. That temptation, by the way, does not consist of sending up my distress signal and throwing in the towel, as one might think. It is the thousand and one little daily temptations that lie in wait for us all: to get out of bed five minutes later than usual; to stop one minute before the bell rings signaling the end of the working day; to pull a trifle less vigorously on the oar next time; even to stop shaving. These are the kinds of minor abandonments, the easings off just a little here and there, which in and of themselves are insignificant but which, taken together, ineluctably lead to the ultimate surrender. And it is these same minor, ridiculous battles, these repetitive, fastidious, inglorious battles that, if I persist, will eventually lead me to victory.

I took out my "seven league boots," my longest oars, each 3.2 meters long, the shafts made of carbon Kevlar, the blades of laminated ash. I had three pairs of oars on board, all different sizes, much as bicycle racers have different gears for different speeds. My various sets of oars enabled me to control my speed depending on the state of the sea and the wind direction. I would use the smallest pair — 3 meters, with smaller blades — when the wind was against me or the sea rough, which, alas, was the case most of the time. But on this day, with a brisk tail wind, the sea was good, so was life, and *Sector* was flying.

To keep a steady course would have been exhausting if that meant constantly correcting course by maneuvering one oar or the other as I rowed. Aboard a sailing craft you can shift the sails and the rudder to keep a steady course, but in a rowboat the matter is slightly more complicated. Your speed is minimal, and too large a rudder would have acted like a brake. The solution: vertical stabilizers that can be raised or lowered as the situation requires. *Sector* had three such stabilizers, two aft — on either side of the rudder blade — and one forward. About ten inches wide, and made of steel, they were set into watertight housings built into the boat between the hull and the deck. I was able to control them by a series of ropes that I could maneuver from the cockpit and could lower them either wholly or partially according to my needs. For example, when there were crosswinds, I would lower the forward stabilizer slightly to compensate for the surface of the rudder and thereby keep a steady course. With the wind behind me, it would be the opposite: I would fully immerse the two aft stabilizers and let the boat run, at the same time bringing the forward stabilizer back into its housing.

Today, that was precisely what was happening.

A real treat! With 100 kilos (more than 200 pounds) of ballast in my after tanks to accentuate the effect of the stabilizers, *Sector* was racing gaily over the bounding main. Three knots an hour easily, sometimes three and a half. By nightfall my speed log had chalked up a good thirty knots, rounding out one of my most successful days.

July 22

Evening: As I write, I can hear the wind rising again. What will the weather be like tomorrow? How strange it is to have only one thought, one simple, overwhelming concern: where will the wind be coming from tomorrow? I think back to my life over these past few months, to the thousand little problems and worries I encountered every day — all seemingly absolutely essential, every one of primary importance, things that loomed so large they would be forever ingrained in my mind. And now the only thing that matters is: where will the wind be coming from?

July 24

Sympathizing with my efforts, God or the devil — I was no longer sure which of the two I was dependent on at this point — shifted the wind a little farther south. I lowered my forward stabilizer, the starboard ballast filled to the brim to keep the boat from listing, and I managed to keep *Sector* heading due north. But the weather conditions were growing worse by the minute.

1305: A birth on board! Upon my opening the sea chest that contains the stock of wine and taking out one of the three oversize containers — one filled with Bordeaux, another with Burgundy, and the third with wine from the Loire Valley — a tiny fly emerges and "escapes." I wish it bon voyage and long life, but I fear that it will be short. The fly who gave it birth chose the wrong spot for its infant.

July 27

In a moment of optimism, I note in my log:

Slightly foggy, smooth sea, a real holiday. I had forgotten that such weather really exists. I'm moving right along thanks to a stiff westerly wind. According to the weather report, the good weather is supposed to last till August 15!

As it turned out, it wouldn't last even for twenty-four hours: the wind was shifting to the south.

I had a long conversation with myself, the pilot charts spread out in front of me. Ideally, my plan had been to profit as long as possible from the beneficial effects of the Kuroshio, but that now seemed questionable. Should I follow the direct route, that is, the ellipsis that marks the shortest route between Japan and the United States? If I did, it would mean I would have to separate myself sooner than I liked from the favorable current and take advantage of the wind by heading northeast.

With the trip scheduled to last four to five months, here I was only in my third week. To be already so far behind schedule made me fear the worst. Scanning the charts, I tried to reason coldly, but what I foresaw was anything but reassuring, as my log for the day testifies:

I'm afraid my arrival is going to be tough, very tough; from September 19 on, and especially in October, the statistics indicate that waves up to ten feet and force-five winds will be the rule rather than the exception. What's more, I'm going to have to navigate very carefully or else I risk not being able to put in at San Francisco. Which means I had better get going as fast as I can.

5

With My Head in the Stars

Finally I ran smack into it. An invisible, moving rampart. The wall of east winds, head winds, diversionary and distracting winds, in the literal sense of the term.

For two weeks, from July 31 to August 14, I did nothing but zigzag back and forth across the ocean, advancing with enormous difficulty when the winds abated, glued to my oars for hours just to make a few miles' progress. Then, during the night, with my sea anchors out, I would drift back that same precious distance under the relentless force of the east winds.

Two weeks of growing depression, in which I saw the summer, or what remained of it, inexorably disappear. Often I consciously decided *not* to check my position, so disgusted was I by the knowledge of what I would most certainly find — that I had lost many degrees of longitude that I had won so dearly only hours or days before.

To reach my goal, I had to create a mental universe wherein my forward progress was king, the only thing that mattered. It was a fragile universe at best: now that I was completely becalmed — two steps forward and two steps back, as it were — the temptation to give up was always with me. I spent hours, days, simply waiting for the wind to shift. To try to overcome my growing despair, I would frequently pull in the sea anchor, strap myself in the cockpit, and row till I dropped, all the while fully aware of how pointless the effort was. But anything that helped me keep alive the notion that I was making progress was good, anything that kept me from dwelling on the worst.

I had no news of my family and friends, whose absence I felt more strongly with every passing day. I had the strange impression of being a speleologist, descending deeper and deeper into the darkness, into the night. During my first several days out I had clung to the memories of my colleagues who had accompanied me to Japan, imagining in exquisite detail everything they might be doing. In my mind I had gone back to France with Bruno and, since I knew what his plans and itinerary were, I went with him to Brittany where I knew he had to pick up his car, then accompanied him as he drove down to southern France. Christopher "served" me for a little longer, since I knew he was staying on in Japan for a week and then joining a mutual friend as navigator on his sailboat. But as time went on, I began to lose them. Solitude closed in around me, real solitude, the kind that disconnects you from the rest of the world.

I'm an old hand at being alone. My experience rowing across the Atlantic had taught me that, when it comes to solitude, the best thing is to dive right in, immerse yourself in it, rather than try to resist it. But at this point things were at a very low ebb. So, any time I took a break I slipped into the cockpit to take a quick look at my ammeter and check the output of my solar panels that were charging my radio batteries. I was obsessed — although I refused to admit it to myself — with the desire for human contact, however superficial, a need so overpowering that it frightened me. My little pill of ephemeral happiness. I desperately needed those terribly brief radio contacts, which broke off far too soon, leaving me each time plunged even deeper in my solitude.

Two weeks after leaving Choshi, I picked up some American voices on my radio. I couldn't believe it! Since then no more contacts. Had it been some quirk of the nocturnal air waves? In any case, just hearing the language of the country of my arrival warmed my heart. Even though I knew in my heart of hearts how far, far off it still was. . . .

The "mystery" was solved on the day when, tuning in to the same frequency, I heard a man saying he planned to spend the weekend in Manila. So my ham radio operator was based in the Philippines. Which immediately gave me a bright idea. Two of my brothers were living there at the time. All I had to do was make contact with this American operator, convince him to telephone one of my brothers and set up a radio appointment with him. That way, I figured, I could perhaps make contact, through him, with my family in France.

"Break!" "Break!"

After a bit of static, the American homed in on my frequency. He must have been a bit taken aback to hear me say, "This is *Sector*, rowboat *Sector*. I'm rowing across the Pacific. You're my first contact in nine days. I wonder if you could telephone my brother?"

I was dying to exchange a few words with Cornélia, to find out how she was and how the children were doing during their summer vacation. Guillaume, I knew, was taking sailing lessons, and I wanted an update on his progress. I also wanted to talk with Christopher, to give him an update. But as it turned out it would be another several weeks before I got through via radio. For that, I had to hook up with a maritime station that would relay the radio call to a telephone network. So far, I hadn't been able to effect that.

All of this brought me back to the telex, which was still giving me fits. Every time I raised the antenna above the cockpit it seemed to suffer from some slight twist or bend inflicted on it. The connection, which was already fragile, seemed to get worse day by day, no matter how carefully I handled it, until one day it snapped altogether. I improvised a makeshift substitute, but to no avail. The machine had made up its mind once and for all that it was not going to work, even if I treated it like the Holy Sacrament. With that machine, I went from one disillusionment to another.

Then one evening there appeared on its little screen the following: MESSAGE RECEIVED. Feverishly, I searched the computer's memory bank. Nothing. And then on the screen there flashed: MESSAGE RECEIVED.

I felt like tossing the damned thing overboard.

"TM6 ABO, TM6 ABO, this is FK8CR calling. Come in TM6 ABO. . . ."

Eddy, a ham radio operator out of Noumea, had just entered my little world. On a regular basis — and for stretches, every day — he brought me both comfort and valuable weather information. FK8CR, Eddy's call sign, was a very sophisticated setup. He had a fax that received from the satellites the full weather report on the Pacific, which he would pass on to me. Till the end of my trip, Eddy remained a staunch and faithful friend, often sacrificing his weekends to keep me up to date on the movement of storms and cyclones, as well as passing on messages from friends.

But right now I really needed help. I had cut back my rations to one meal a day. Given all my "lost days," days with little or no progress, I knew there was a growing risk that I would run out of food. Increasingly, I was assailed by doubts. The successful outcome of the crossing seemed to me less and less certain.

The minute the vice that held me in its grip slackened a bit and I saw an opening, I took up my oars and rowed steadily, hoping to break the vicious cycle of row and drift. But again the winds would rise, often to gale fury, and drive me back into the cabin for safety, with sea anchors out to mitigate the damage. And there I would huddle like some caged beast as the waves hammered me and the gale winds whistled, waiting for the boat to capsize.

In situations such as that, a living hell, there is no way you can force your mind to take refuge in other thoughts because it, too, is a prisoner of the unpredictable, convulsive movements of the boat and can focus on nothing else.

I thought of the First World War, of the soldiers burrowed in their trenches, who could tell simply by the whine of the shell what caliber it was. And there I was, hunkered down in my cabin, listening for the roar of the waves, trying to guess which one it would be that would capsize the boat. There were times when this went on for a ten-hour stretch.

As if by chance, at this juncture my first physical problems surfaced. One morning when I woke up, I felt a stabbing pain behind my left shoulder, in a spot where it was of course impossible for me to rub in any salve. But sometimes misfortune has its virtues. The weather was so bad it forced me to keep the sea anchors out and take the day off. I kept to my cabin all day and used the time to clean and disinfect every little cut and bruise I had — an indispensable precaution at sea where the slightest scratch or abrasion can quickly get infected. At last I had a moment to take care of myself physically. But from a morale viewpoint, there was no medicine on board to heal me.

August 10

Believe it or not, a telex arrived from Cornélia. The machine I had given up on actually funtioned. It was my first news from her since my departure, and I was delighted to get it. But it also left me terribly frustrated. She hadn't given me enough details. She told me that she and the children had gone out to dinner at a restaurant. But what restaurant? Where? Had she driven there? By what route? I wanted the name of the restaurant, what table they had, what the menu was. I was starved for details. Here I lacked everything. Everything that had a smell, a color, a special flavor. Did she have any idea how frustrating it was to be deprived of these tiny, simple parts of life? Could she have any notion of how badly I needed to feel them, touch them, breathe them?

August 11

During the night, tremendous battering by the waves. A low pressure system must have passed through directly above me. The wind suddenly shifted 180 degrees; the sea was raging.

I put out two sea anchors from the bow, which did not prevent *Sector* from being knocked about like a cork. Inside my watertight cabin I had the feeling, through the "skin" of the hull, that I was being beaten, soundly thrashed, throughout the night.

But the following morning I awoke to a pleasant surprise. A northwest wind had dissipated the nightmare. I pulled myself out of the cabin, my arms and legs stiff and numb. My eyes were wide with disbelief: could the winds really have shifted in my favor?

The bad news was that though the wind was now in the

right direction, it was still strong, and the sea was still raging. The idea of leaving my dry lair and getting soaked in the cockpit did not exactly delight me. Yet doing nothing was even worse. I started by pulling in the sea anchors, letting *Sector* run with the wind, and proceeded to tidy up both the boat and myself, as if it were Sunday morning on a pleasure craft. A dab of grease on any point where rust had begun to appear, then a shave, a bit of fresh water on my face, my hair combed. . . . Feeling much better, I climbed into the cockpit, took up the oars, and rowed for the next nine hours straight, directly northeast.

August 14

Clear blue sky, such as I had very rarely seen since my departure. Yet the barometer was falling rapidly. Did that mean I was finally getting the low pressure system that had been predicted? I realized I had just regained the position I had reached back on July 31. Two weeks of no progress!

Where were those little squeaking sounds coming from? From the computer? My quartz watch? I was in the cabin having lunch when I first heard the strange, high-pitched noises. I checked the computer, listened to my watch, checked all the equipment — nothing out of the ordinary. Looking further, I discovered that a school of dolphins, probably a hundred or so, were frolicking not far off, and as they swam and dove their high-pitched cries were reverberating underwater and bouncing off my hull.

* * *

My boils were not causing me too much trouble. In fact, to date I had not had much to complain about as far as my health was concerned. I had kept in fairly close radio contact with Dr. Chauve, whose task it was to advise me on any health problems I encountered. But I knew myself well enough to know that the poor man would have had a serious problem fulfilling his role of medical guardian angel, because when I do have a health problem of any sort, I prefer not to mention it, or if I do, it will be only in passing. Even when, later on in the crossing, I would break two ribs and a finger, I could see no point in dwelling on it. Of course, it was painful, but I also knew it was not life-threatening, that it was something I could cope with. As long as I was able to keep on rowing, nothing else mattered to me. To make lengthy notations in my log or over the radio about my health would only have worried my family and friends unnecessarily and also have provided me with ready excuses for giving up if my mind began to crack or my resolve began to weaken.

August 17

Two weeks behind in my game plan. I had to increase my daily rowing schedule.

Under normal conditions, that is, when the weather was not bad enough to keep me from rowing, my day began at first light. Up at 0600. I gulp down my breakfast, a high-energy concoction of dried fruit and cereal washed down with a cup of hot chocolate or coffee. I take a quick look outside. At dawn or dusk the color of the sky can give me a pretty good idea what to expect over the next few hours. A technicolor dawn is a bad sign; on the other hand, a brilliant sundown bodes well.

After heating up the coffee, I set it down in the cockpit. This is a none too subtle way of forcing myself to leave the relative comfort of the cabin, since I have a tendency to go where the coffee is. . . . "Here in the cockpit," I keep telling myself, "is where the action is." And so my day begins.

I row from 0630 to 0930 without pause. Then I take a break to have a cup of coffee or a bowl of hot soup, and it's back to the grind for another couple of hours, roughly till noon. I take a midday break of an hour and a half or two hours — in good French fashion — for lunch, to check my position with sextant and charts, and, upon occasion, to smoke a small cigar. From 1400 to 1600 hours, back to the cockpit and another two hours' steady rowing. A further short break, then a third stint at the oars till 2000. Whenever I'm forced to put out the sea anchors and stay inside — whether for a few hours or in some cases for several days in a row — I make up for it by extending those "normal" hours and rowing late into the night.

If I kept religiously to that schedule, that golden rule, it was because I knew that if I were to let up, stray from it for even a few extra minutes, I ran the danger of growing more lax every day and, finally, giving up.

When I had a good day — and you can translate that quite simply into a day when I made good forward progress — my morale was high and my appetite good. Aside from my canned goods, I fed myself essentially on the dried concentrate that so impressed the Japanese customs officials. It's not as bad as it sounds: when you add some water and heat it up, it's really quite palatable. The advantages of the concentrate: it's extremely nourishing, therefore keeps your weight up; no problem of preservation; reasonably good taste. The disadvantage: after several weeks at sea, it all begins to taste the same. But I told myself that if I had steak every day for four months I'd probably get tired of it, too. Not completely convincing!

Speaking of steak, the dried steaks I had on board required, after the water had been added, being cooked in a frying pan, for which you needed a bit of cooking fat. Shortly before my departure, I discovered in a store that specialized in camping equipment a kind of fat concentrate, which unfortunately I had not had the time to test. It looked like the tiny soap pellets you see in swanky bathrooms, more for decorative than practical purposes. In the frying pan the melted substance looked like ordinary cooking fat. But *caveat eater*: when it cools, the ersatz matter quickly reverts to its original consistency, which means that unless you eat your steak with considerable speed, you find your jaws slowing with each bite as the waxlike substance takes command. Fortunately, I had brought along with me a number of canned goods, identical to those I had on board the *Captain Cook,* to supplement my nourishing but wearisome concentrates. Among them was tuna fish packed in olive oil. I guarded the olive oil preciously: it made all the difference in cooking my steaks!

A key element for my survival were the desalination pumps. Eleven years ago when I crossed the Atlantic, there were no such pumps; I had to carry with me no less than three hundred liters of liquid, including water and wine. The liquid weighed more than the boat itself. For the Pacific, I would have had to take on at least five hundred liters. Fortunately, over the intervening years, compact pumps were invented, whereby seawater could be turned into drinking water using a system of filters. Some pumps, which have been tested aboard sailing ships around the world, are electric and can purify considerable quantities of water a day. Other models, intended primarily for lifeboats, are manually operated.

My pump weighed a scant eight-and-a-half pounds, and in twelve minutes I could produce about a liter of water. Since I consumed no more than a liter and a half a day, that pump more than sufficed my needs, but for safety's sake I had another, identical model on board, plus an additional pump, which worked on a slightly different principle. A submersible pump, it utilized the pressure of the water itself to operate the piston forcing water into the filter. Since its output was less than that of the other two, I used it rarely, but just having it on board provided me with a certain comfort.

One of my brilliant, energy-saving ideas when the boat was being rigged was to utilize the movement of the rowing seat to activate the desalination pumps as I rowed. Though it was my idea, it was Bruno who had the technical ability to translate it into reality by installing a simple mechanism under the seat linking pump and seat. But once again harsh reality took its toll: in order to activate the pump, I found I had to row at a pace faster than I was comfortable with, and in the long run it wore me out. Another factor was that on bad days, when I couldn't row at all, the system was useless. So I quickly reverted to the hand-pump.

Though in crossing the Atlantic I had taken on board a fair amount of wine — as any Frenchman worthy of the name would have done — I did so on the reasonably sound theory that the more wine I took the less water would be needed, since liter for liter they weighed the same. But with my desalination pumps, I had had a real battle with my conscience: one liter of wine was roughly two pounds' additional weight.

After wrestling with my soul, I did include twelve liters of wine among my provisions, judging that minimal quantity absolutely essential to my morale. A half-glass of wine with every meal made all the difference in the world, especially when it was consumed in a proper wine glass, another slight indulgence. I coddled that goblet as though it were the family jewels, but despite all my efforts I ultimately lost it to the elements. The victim of one of the many times the boat capsized, it shattered into a thousand pieces.

August 18

This morning, a sobering realization. I have only covered one fourth of my route! And it has taken me 38 days. . . . At that rate, the whole crossing will take a little more than five months. . . . All of which leaves me pensive, and my morale sagging. I will have to consider rationing my food even further.

At 0500 I climbed into the cockpit, took up the oars, and tried to head northwest. Compass. Speed log. Always the same old story. The same metronomelike cadence. The shoulder, the arm, the hand, the oar form one single, homogenous member, perfectly adapted to its function. My nerves begin at the tip of the blades. In the heavy swells and crosscurrents, those members control the strokes: lift and lose a stroke to keep the oar from breaking, correct the angle of the oar striking the water, pull a trifle harder on the starboard oar to correct the bow's heading by three or four degrees.

The body functions like a machine and the mind like a calculator. Averages . . . number of days . . . keeping accounts. I constantly tried to estimate my time of crossing,

reassessing and recalculating, examining all the probabil-
ities, forever extrapolating. On good days, I tried to make
forty nautical miles, which is one degree of longitude. That
was my point of reference. My mind was filled with figures;
figures filled my notebooks, columns of figures that a strong
gust of wind could wipe out in a second.

For hours on end as I rowed, I would concentrate on my
secret calculations. My projections were that, at best, I
would reach land between November 10 and 15. At worst,
December 15.

The moment I most looked forward to every day was when
I plotted my exact position. My instruments told me precisely where I was in relation to the stars and the satellites.
I found a certain fascination, almost a giddiness, in meas-
uring my infinitesimal progress thanks to these cosmic bea-
cons. My feet were firmly planted in my miniscule cockpit,
but through the lens of my sextant, my head was in the
stars, and the scope of my mind expanded then to universal
dimensions.

And yet, what did my mind really focus on, sometimes
to the point of obsession: things of human dimension —
sounds, smells, familiar places.

What a paradox!

My penury helped me to rediscover the importance of
everything one no longer sees, because I was so close
to it.

6

And If All This Were Really Pointless

August 19

This ocean is pitiless, by its size alone. If this were the Atlantic, and I had already covered the same distance, I would already be halfway across. Here, when I look at my map, I'm still so damnably close to Japan. . . .

I try not to count in days any longer but count in weeks, even in months. Alas, when I'm rowing, though, I count in hours, in quarter hours, sometimes in minutes. I have such a double concept of time: one that concerns my crossing, where I count in weeks — the other my day, where I count in minutes.

Glued to my seat, dazed and deadened by this automaton's toil, I tried not to look at my watch too often. In keeping with the rules I had laid down for myself, I allowed myself five minutes respite every hour, every full hour. So I watched the minute hand crawl slowly on its appointed rounds, ever so slowly, as though it were stuck. Time seemed to slow down with every successive stroke of the oars, and the upcoming stroke seemed ever so much harder than the one before. Each minute lasted an hour, each hour a day. Six hours of rowing and only five knots on the speed log wasn't much forward progress. But I felt so much better in the cockpit than bored to death back in the cabin.

I was obsessed by the passing of the season. It was terrible, this sword of Damocles constantly hanging over my head, moving ever closer as the weather conditions worsened and as, inexorably, the storms became more frequent, longer, and more dangerous.

August 20

Ideal weather, after a long period of dull days. The nights were clear, but the days dragged on in endless successions of pale gray, which meant that my telex was out, since the solar panels were generating no electricity. With the sun out again, my batteries were recharging, and I could at long last send some messages.

I heard a number of transmissions on my ham radio wavelengths, from Pacific Net, a network out of Hawaii, and tonight, for the first time, I also picked up a ham radio out of San Jose, California. Now that made me feel as if I were actually closing the gap.

I was in an area of high pressure systems. Foul winds, which created crosscurrents. I needed to move north, into higher latitudes. And there, I knew, bad weather awaited me. What a terrible paradox: go where the bad weather is, because there you can make better progress!

Several transpacific jets, arcing high overhead. Doubtless they were following the jet streams, those tailwinds you pick up at altitudes of between 25,000 and 40,000 feet, which for the pilots meant cutting a good twenty minutes off their flight times. When I thought of that other world, so near and yet so far and different, of those passengers comfortably ensconced in their seats directly over my head, I had a very strange feeling. A combination of envy and indifference.

The Pacific is incredibly empty. In the course of more than a month I only encountered two ships. One was the car carrier *Nissan,* which looked like an enormous, floating parking lot, filled to capacity with brand-new cars. They are the ugliest boats I've ever seen: only by really examining them closely can you tell which end is the stern and which the bow. The second encounter was a Chinese ship — with which I established brief radio contact — on its way to the Columbia River estuary in Oregon.

What a contrast with the "little" Atlantic, which is so much busier when it comes to traffic. During my earlier trip I had run into a German passenger liner — which I actually boarded, having accepted the captain's invitation for coffee — but I had also crossed paths with a Russian trawler, a Norwegian freighter, the French weather ship *France II,* a tuna fishing vessel, and a number of others. Here in the Pacific, fellow mariners were scarce as hen's teeth.

I could count on the fingers of one hand the number of sunny days I'd had since I set out. I was voyaging through a lugubrious, monochrome world. And where oh where were the fish? The only signs of animal life to date: a mosquito, a fly, and a few dolphins who came and took shelter next to my hull. Plus, one suspicious-looking fin and, on another occasion, the back of a whale. The whale's appearance was so brief that by the time I got my camera, in the hope of recording its presence, it was already gone.

Then all of a sudden, I saw another whale. *Sector* cleared the decks for action! The cetacean seemed huge, a full thirty-plus feet from snout to dorsal fin, as far as I could judge from my position. The creature was swimming about one hundred yards directly in front of *Sector*'s bow. Feverishly, I got out my camera to record the rare event in this endless seascape. The whale was too far away to get a meaningful picture. I slapped the water with the blade of my oar, since I had always been told that that makes them come. Nothing. The whale was ignoring me completely. Irritated, I took to the oars and tried to overtake it, to no avail: it turned its back and sounded, with a movement of its tail that was both majestic and disdainful. Later — this was unquestionably my day for social calls — a band of dolphins appeared to starboard, and I was delighted to receive them. It reminded me of the times when I used to sail with Cornélia on the *Lady Maud,* when dolphins would appear by the dozens and play and frolic in the wake of our boat. Their northern Pacific brethren apparently had no desire to waste their time with a playmate as slow and clumsy as *Sector.* I felt like shouting to them, "Hey, guys! I exist, too, you know!"

August 23

A close call — no, a hair's breadth from death. I had been standing on the deck trying to screw back in the upper part of the antenna when it broke off at the point part way up where it screws into the base, causing me to lose my balance. I did not have my safety harness on, and almost fell overboard. I grabbed hold for dear life, and came out of the fall with no more than a black-and-blue bruise and an awful scare. The boat was drifting rapidly; had I fallen, there would have been no way I could ever have caught up with it.

One bad reflex, and it could have been all over.

August 24

A terrible day.

This morning, at 0630, while I was still in the cabin, a huge wave hit Sector *broadside and capsized it.*

For an hour I had worked to right the boat, without success. I tried every combination I could think of: emptying and filling the various ballast tanks, shifting my weight from one side of the hull to the other . . . nothing worked.

I was sweating like a pig, and I also knew I was running out of air. I had more and more trouble breathing, and I could feel my heart beating crazily, uncontrollably. It was a downward cycle: the more upset I became, the harder it was to breathe and the faster my heart beat. I unhooked the speedometer screw, to create a tiny opening in the hull above me and, I hoped, let in a little air. Water trickled in and I could feel a tiny bit of air as well, but not enough to do me much good. The atmosphere in the cabin was still stifling. I had no other choice but to leave the cabin. It was a desperate move, because once the cabin was flooded I had no idea whether I would ever be able to turn the craft back over from the outside. I ran through the exercise in my mind, over and over again. I prepared to send up my distress signal, which was strapped to my thigh. To emerge from the cabin backward would be especially difficult, since I would end up in the cockpit of a capsized boat that was being battered by the waves, a boat bobbing about in every direction. Even the very thought terrified me. But I was

more frustrated at the thought of being trapped in the
cabin. . . .

A miracle. About 0815, the boat finally turned back over.

I had been in the capsized cabin for an hour and forty-
five minutes. For the next two hours I lay on my bunk in
a state of complete collapse, trying to get my wits about
me again but incapable of doing anything whatsoever.

I set off rowing. The ocean was still raging, and I managed
to ride the waves at speeds of up to twelve knots. It was
sheer folly — and very dangerous — to row in this weather,
but I was overcome with an irresistible need to banish the
terrible claustrophobia I had gone through earlier in the
day.

Suddenly the boat capsized again. I was caught in the
cockpit, all tangled up in my safety harness. I fought like
a tiger to get loose. As the boat bobbed about, I was able
to get my head out of water, on one side or the other, and
breathe in a lungful or two of air, then go under again. I
had also swallowed a great deal of water. The boat was
bouncing about, and I was being struck every time it
moved. A nightmare. In the midst of the welter of white
water and foam, I kept struggling to unbuckle my safety
harness. But I could feel my strength fading, second by
second. I could see the end. Then, just as I was about to
give up, I managed to wrench myself free. I was near the
end of my strength. I knew I still had to drag myself to the
stern post, holding on to the rigging. . . . *Sector* was drifting
at high speed. If my fingers ever lost their grip, there was
no way I would ever get back to the boat. Hanging on to
the rudder, I hoisted myself up onto the hull with the last
bit of energy I could muster. There, straddling the hull,

which was as slippery as it was unstable, I managed to make my way to the middle. The anchor rope, attached to the deck beneath me, was floating in the waves, and I latched on to it with my toes, pulled it in with all my remaining strength, and finally managed to turn *Sector* back over again. Except that now it was right on top of me. I didn't have the strength to climb back on board. I kept hold of the anchor rope, meanwhile trying to fill my lungs with air and my body, I hoped, with renewed strength. I hoisted one foot into the cockpit, then a full leg, then the rest of me. I collapsed there, unable to move, and threw up.

1730: I'm completely exhausted, and very demoralized. . . . I know that wisdom and common sense are both telling me to throw in the towel. I also know that I can't bring myself to take that step until I am compelled to. And when that happens, will I still have time to make the choice? I am well aware that earlier today I was at death's door.

August 25

Ate almost nothing yesterday or all day today. Last night I didn't sleep a wink, still under the effect of the day's traumatic events. Found myself gasping for breath a number of times. I had battened down everything for obvious reasons, and when I had trouble breathing I took a quick tour outside and the problem ceased immediately. Probably the foul air of the cabin.

A feeling of not being able to breathe. The first time the boat capsized was more traumatizing than the second, when I had to do something, and do it fast. But yesterday morning, when I'd suddenly found myself imprisoned underneath the boat, caught in my safety harness, almost asphyxiated, my heart pounding uncontrollably, I was like an animal caught in a trap.

The greatest danger was to feel sorry for yourself: a moment of weakness. It was not even a question of being tempted to give up, of sending up the distress signal and being picked up by a ship, but a matter of letting yourself die, of saying to yourself: "It's just too hard, I've capsized one more time, one time too many. I'm giving up and letting go." Stupidly. Because at some given moment it would be easier to throw in the towel than continue fighting.

In 1980, when I rowed across the Atlantic, there were three of us who were making the solo attempt. The other two didn't make it. Disappeared. I think I know when and how that happened, the storm that did them in. That kind of depression, of complete distress, with your boat overturned and righted with God-knows-what difficulty, then overturned again: you feel you just can't cope anymore. Obviously, those are the times when your adventure — and you yourself — are at greatest risk.

The second time I capsized, there was a partial sun, and that helped. Had the same thing happened at night, I don't know what might have happened.

I have experienced those moments of depression, those periods of discouragement when your morale gets shaky, and all your thoughts are negative. There were times when I was so tired and disgusted that I began to cry. I had the impression that what I was doing was ridiculous. Normally, I'm the kind of person who reacts positively to serious situations. But when I emerged from those nightmarish hours, knowing perfectly well that in the days and weeks to come there would very likely be situations even worse, even more unbearable, the thought crossed my mind: "And what if all this were really pointless? What if I were nothing but a clown, a seafaring buffoon, the way there are land-lubber clowns and buffoons everywhere, then what's the point of all this, what is this madness to survive all about?"

The answers, or what seemed to be the answers, to those questions would only become clear at the end of my trip. Because I would have stayed the course, given my all, body and soul, to accomplish my goal: to have rowed across that ocean, having done it in my mind a hundred times, maybe a thousand, both before and during my crossing. I had the bit between my teeth, and I was gripping it, harder and harder.

One evening, picking up a French Radio broadcast, I learned that a typhoon had hit Bangladesh and devastated it. The human toll was in the dozens, maybe even hundreds. And only a few short weeks earlier that ravaged land had already suffered the death of thousands of its people. That day I made the following entry in my log:

Isn't it an incredible luxury to have undertaken this cross-ing? I gave up all the modern comforts I could have en-joyed, of my own free will, put my life at risk when so many others around the world are battling fiercely simply to survive, to find enough to eat one more day. I under-stand that some might view my endeavor as the epitome of self-indulgence, even indecency. But who knows, even in an area as impoverished and ravaged as Bangladesh, whether there aren't some youngsters who are dreaming of one day accomplishing some extraordinary — and per-haps "useless" — exploit.

August 26

A dragonfly in the cockpit! Where in the world could it have come from? It looked to me completely groggy. Maybe a storm had driven it skyward from somewhere on the Kamchatka peninsula and flung it miles and miles through the heavens till it found me here in the middle of the ocean. I picked it up, but when I tried to feed it a little sugary water, it got scared and flew off.

1630: The boat has capsized again.
The wave was violent enough to snap off the radio antenna. I was able to right the craft in five minutes, without too much difficulty. I fashioned a makeshift antenna so as not to miss my evening session with my ham radio pal.

Very faint contact with Eddy — FK8CR — but nonetheless enough for him to read me two messages, one from Cornélia, the other from Guillaume. For the last several days my solar panels were not recharging my batteries, or at best ever so slightly. It pained me to think that these were perhaps their last messages.

That night, despite the heavy sea, I filled my ballast tanks to the top, and put the sea anchors out, to prevent *Sector* from being swallowed up by the waves.

The boat was being picked up by the terrifying swells and lifted for what seemed the equivalent of several stories high in the space of five to ten seconds. Then it was hurled forward by the wave, descending into the trough at the speed of madness. If it took a real nosedive, there was a good chance it would do a somersault. I bunked down with my head facing the stern, to minimize the risk of having it banged against the compartment bulkhead. This time I got through the night without breaking anything. But, I kept thinking, how long before my luck ran out?

101

August 28

Another capsizing this morning. But with no real problems.
So that makes five.

August 29

Evening. Tonight I succeeded in making telephone contact
with my parents in Kérantré, thanks to the intermediary
of a Japanese maritime station. The connection was poor,
full of static and echoes, but I did manage to exchange a
few words with my father and also with Guillaume, who
just happened to be there. They couldn't believe their ears.
To boot, all that took place during a beautiful night, filled
with the soft glow of the moon.

August 31

Superb day, sun virtually throughout, good session of
rowing, naked for several hours. . . . If only winter never
came, and if I weren't such a poor wretched creature out
here in the middle of the Pacific, life would be a bowl of
cherries!

I found a fish in the cockpit, a good twelve inches long.
Perfectly edible. I served it for lunch. And besides, it was
Friday.

In the early stages of the crossing, a few fish had swum
along beside me, using my hull as a moving shelter. During
the Atlantic crossing, they had been my personal reserve,
a refrigerator into which I could dip virtually at will.

But here in the Pacific they very quickly spurned my company, doubtless heading for warmer waters.

This fish, fallen like manna from heaven, would be my only catch of the entire crossing. I had already lost all my fishing gear, which had been stored in the cockpit in a sea chest whose lock had broken during one of the times the boat had turned over. In any event, I had a feeling that the equipment would not have done me much good: these waters were apparently lifeless.

On this ocean, where I encountered so few signs of life, the traces of my fellow man were nonetheless very much in evidence. Pollution was visible everywhere. I am not referring to those signs of terrible and perhaps irremediable pollution, such as the oil spills from the gigantic tankers, but of a rampant ordinary pollution that revealed itself in countless little ways: plastic bags, Styrofoam packing, et cetera.

Every twenty minutes or so I would come upon some sort or another of debris, which, considering my limited horizon, suggests the magnitude of the problem: I could only imagine the mountain it would all make were it gathered together and piled up. Worse, I knew that most of this detritus was indestructible, and that each year a new batch was added to that of the previous year. What irony, when you think that these were not even the waste products of human consumption but merely the packing material in which they had come! To be sure, this petty pollution did not have the same devastating effect on the environment that the oil spills did, but it still was a terrible feeling for me to find this in the midst of what should have been the great pristine sea. I felt a little like a mountain climber who finally reaches the top of Mount Everest only to discover a bevy of beer cans. None of that diminished the difficulty of my task, but it did slightly tarnish the dream.

The only point of interest of this situation: I began to sift through the garbage, looking for something useful. This morning I fished out a large parallelepiped of plastic, which, once it was securely fastened to the deck, might help me right the boat when next it capsized.

I also fished out a buoy. Clinging to it was a tiny crab, which reminded me of the Little Prince on his planet. I invited the crab on board and offered it a bit of dehydrated rice, which it seemed to enjoy immensely.

In the course of the afternoon, I put a message in a bottle and set it adrift. During the Atlantic crossing, I had dropped three empty rum bottles into the sea, each with the same message. I'd never received a reply to my communication efforts in the Atlantic, so I hoped this time the results might be different. In my message I promised the person who found and returned it a reward of $100. Much to my surprise, I had not one but two responses. At the end of my trip, the large-circulation French photo magazine *Paris-Match* published a picture I had taken of the message before I cast it into the sea. On the photo was my home address. A short time later, I received from Venezuela a copy of my message written on lined paper. Pretty smart. Another clever kid from Africa also sent me a letter claiming the reward: all he had done was cut out the picture from *Paris-Match* and pin it to his letter. I sent it back to him with a photograph of a hundred dollar bill. One good photo deserves another!

*　　*　　*

When my trip was over, I received some four thousand letters. Most of them, to my astonishment, and in contrast to the letters I received after my Atlantic crossing, simply said thank you rather than "congratulations" or "bravo," which was the most frequent message of those earlier letters. The first time I read a letter that began by thanking me, I thought it was an exception. But after the tenth, then the hundredth, I began to wonder. Thanks for what? When I set out from Choshi, my goal had not been altruistic. I'm not a guru by any manner of means. I have no message to deliver. No light to shine upon the world. And yet, as I read on, day after day, I realized that despite myself I had given hope to all kinds of people: prisoners, the unemployed, the downtrodden, the homeless. I had touched the lives of people who, for whatever reason, were depressed and discouraged. And, I also saw, I had brought a ray of hope and sunshine into the lives of the aged, those who so often were, as I had been, distressingly alone.

Here is an extract of one letter, from a man doing time:

> For 134 days you gave me, and a lot of the guys in here, I am sure, an incredible boost in morale. I have to tell you, when the news came through that you had landed, I blubbered like a baby. I saw you live, on TV. I couldn't believe your strength, your courage. You had a dream and made it happen, and for us, the unfortunate victims of the judicial system, it was as though you had made our dreams come true, too.
>
> When you said to that television reporter, "We're not all idiots," I laughed. And, believe me, in prison we don't laugh a lot.

Then there was the owner of a little store in our neighborhood who saw Cornélia one day in late autumn, not long before the end of my trip, and said to her: "You know,

105

you're lucky to find me still in business. Things were so slow, I was having such a hard time making ends meet, that I'd just about decided to give up and close the shop. And then, day after day, I started following the radio reports of your husband's progress. What he's doing is incredible. Do you know what — if I'm still open, it's because of him. He gave me courage. I said to myself, if he can make it, so can I. So I held on. My confidence came back. And today I have the absolute conviction that I am going to make it. And he will, too, I'm sure of it."

Throughout my trip there were a hundred times when I couldn't refrain from telling myself: this whole thing is pointless. Well, I was wrong. "This whole thing" did serve a purpose. The simple fact that an ordinary man, endowed with normal physical capabilities, outfitted with simple means, should make an effort to push himself to the limits of his ability — and maybe well beyond — seemed to inspire a great many people, giving them renewed courage and energy to do the same. I had succeeded; why shouldn't they?

The discovery that people were identifying with me did raise some questions of conscience in my mind. You have to be very careful in situations where people look at you as some kind of role model. Too many public adventures have dubious motives, too many causes are subverted and undermined. But when I think back (and I do think back, every day since I've landed, and doubtless will do so for the next ten years), when each stroke of the oars has found its place in my mind, when all that happened has been decanted, pondered, sifted through — if, then, I will have proved that you can fulfill your personal goals by digging deep into your own inner resources, that is already something.

106

The other side of that coin, of course, is that if I'd failed, those who had put their hope and trust in me might have become discouraged, too. But, judging by the enormous amount of interest my exploit aroused even before my departure, and certainly before the outcome was known, I told myself that the very act of trying, of daring, even if the exploit had failed, could well have positive repercussions.

7

Survival

September 2

Another day that was almost my last. I had nonetheless promised myself, after *Sector* capsized on August 3 — the time I was caught outside the cabin when the wave hit — that I would do everything in my power to avoid such a mortally dangerous situation in the future. When the weather was really rough, I absolutely had to remain inside, limiting my trips outside to only the most indispensable maneuvers and regulating the sea anchors.

How can I explain what happened? Was it that I was simply tired of spending the entire morning locked up in the cabin? The need to do something? The enticing call of a ray of sun? Whatever it was, I decided to go into the cockpit and take some photos with my waterproof camera.

Scarcely had I closed the cabin door when a giant wave hit the boat broadside and knocked it over.

I was slightly stunned by the blow. The overturned hull lay next to me. In vain I tried to grab the handrail, but it was too far below the surface. Each time a new wave hit, it lifted the boat broadside and brought it down on top of me. Unless I did something drastic, I realized that I was either going to drown or be knocked unconscious. I figured my only hope was to get myself to the other side of the boat, and the only way I could do that would be to duck under it and come up on the far side. The danger there was that I might get entangled in my safety harness, or get it caught underneath, and never make it to the other side. Which meant that I would have to unfasten my harness. And that in turn meant that if I made the slightest error, the tiniest miscalculation, it would be all over, for *Sector* was drifting much faster than I could swim. I took a deep breath and, between two waves, ducked under the cockpit.

Now on the good side, I groped my way to the stern, all the while hanging on to the handrail. As I had done before, I hoisted myself up onto the hull, using the rudder for support. Then I managed to haul in my camera, which was floating on the waves and — a safety precaution I always followed — was securely fastened to my wrist. Even as I was still cursing myself for having ever allowed such a situation to occur, especially for such a ridiculous reason, I took a picture of the overturned hull. Even if the photo wasn't wonderful, I couldn't help thinking, What an extraordinary document!

I still had to turn the boat back over, which I did by the method I had used the previous time, that is by slipping a rope around the craft and flipping it.

Another close call . . .

I realize that for someone reading this the idea of taking pictures under such circumstances must seem absurd. I see it somewhat differently: such an act of apparent madness may well have been my way of minimizing or undercutting moments that were truly dramatic or even life-threatening. There were many times after the boat had capsized and I was struggling to man the pumps, furiously filling and emptying the ballast tanks in an effort to turn *Sector* right-side up, when I would pause and take a picture of myself, holding the camera out at arm's length.

I am sure that, in these situations of danger and extreme tension, taking a picture was a means of reassuring myself that I still believed in my future. Looking back, the photos would be no more than records of unhappy memories, a means I had used to brave the present, to write my own story. And besides, when you think about it, if I was taking a picture, did that not imply that things were not as bad as they seemed?

My relationship with the video camera was quite different. Although my Sony camera was also in a watertight case, it took a fair amount of tinkering before it was ready to shoot. That meant I could use it only in fair weather, because when the weather was foul I had my hands full just coping with the basic problems of navigation. There was another difference, too: whereas a still photo can capture and express a fleeting emotion, the video camera presupposes a certain degree of "acting." Frankly, I found it difficult to be constantly natural when I was filming myself. Also, my less than ample stock of both batteries and cassettes meant that I could use the video only sparingly, for very specific purposes and on very special occasions.

Early in the trip I had found filming a pleasant diversion, but as time went on and my patience grew thin, I almost came to resent it: every hour lost struck me as unbearable.

September 3

An afternoon of nightmares. The boat has capsized three times. During one of them, I lose the bottom part of the antenna, which I had kept in an "up" position, believing it to be truly indestructible.

Sector was flying. Really running. The waves arrived with a huge roar and hurtled the boat forward at a speed of from fifteen to twenty knots. When all went well, the prow rose up and the boat rode with the wave, but sometimes the wave would crest with the tip of the prow up in the air, and then we would race down and hit the trough as though we were running into a brick wall. The shock of the water against the bulkhead was incredible; the boat would literally stop in its tracks and shudder from stem to stern. Not only would everything in the cabin be propelled forward, but sometimes the boat would capsize.

Each time it did I was dealt a new hand of pain, anxiety, and uncertainty. Once the stanchion that held the frame of my bunk snapped, dropping the bunk to the deck. Another time, the netting that held my clothes in place came loose while the boat was overturned, so that I found myself holding the clothes with one hand — trying to keep them from spilling out — and pumping with the other. Still another time the plastic piece I'd fished from the sea and fastened to the deck ripped, and, in its new position, made it impossible for me to right *Sector*. I could see it through one of the portholes, and there was nothing I could do about it. As luck would have it, a giant wave came along and, for once, lent me a hand by righting *Sector* for me.

My greatest fear was being thrown off the boat. If that were to happen, I knew that I would have neither the time nor the possibility of sending any message. My distress signal, which sends signals via satellites, would be inoperable. Back on land, there would be no radio communication, but that would not necessarily be taken as an indication of disaster, since I had forewarned my family and colleagues that there might be times when the weather would prevent

111

my solar batteries from recharging and prevent radio contact perhaps for days, even weeks on end. Until they received my distress signal, there was no reason to worry.

What upset me most in that context was the thought that
my family would inevitably keep hoping and believing that
I was all right, knowing that I had enough food supplies on
board to last me several months. There is nothing worse
than a "disappearance." I was haunted by that thought,
that vision of my family waiting, waiting, their spirits
buoyed by false hopes.

I am not the sort of person who dwells interminably on the
whys and hows of any given situation, who contemplates
philosophical minutiae and anguishes over them for long
periods. Rather, I have a tendency to say: "Instead of ques-
tioning why you're doing something, what it will result in
or bring you, or what you might lose by not doing it, for
God's sake, just do it." The act of doing is pretty good in
and of itself. If answers are required, they will follow in
their own good time. For me, reflection is born of action.
I am not one of those philosophers in an ivory tower who
develops an idea based on either the affirmations of the
society in which he lives or on the theories of his fellow-
philosophers. No. Practical applications are what interest
me, even if I subsequently find that the water in which I
swam was only lukewarm. I just can't get away from this
damned need for independence!

When the effort, or the undertaking, takes place on as
demanding a level as this one, there is no question but that
the enormous sense of accomplishment, the dangers faced,
the anguish dealt with, the very fact that you have lived
with, brushed up against death, time and time again, all
give birth to a thousand thoughts, a thousand subjects of

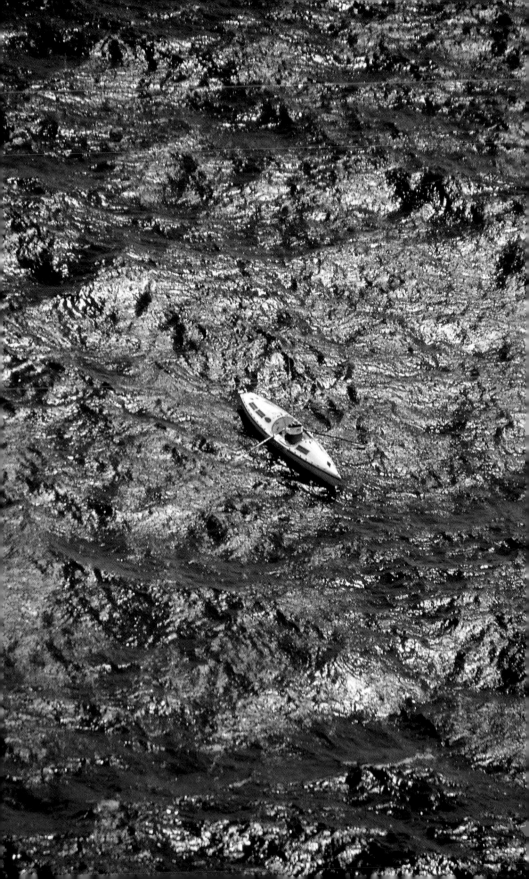

CAPITAINE COOK

September 20, 1980. After my 72-day voyage across the Atlantic Ocean, from Cape Cod in Massachusetts to the entrance of the English Channel, this picture of me and my trusty *Captain Cook* was taken as I was pulling into the little port of Brest, in France. *Jean Guichard/Sygma.*

Preceding page: An aerial view of *Sector*, taken from a helicopter shortly before my arrival on American soil. *Gilles Klein/Sipa Sport.*

All the cargo and equipment I took on board . . .
1. A pair of oars. 2. Clothing. 3. Dehydrated food (125 kilograms or about 275 pounds). 4. Tank of gas. 5. High-energy foods. 6. Captain Cook–brand canned food (25 kilograms or about 55 pounds). 7. Satellite position finder. 8. Books. 9. Plastic bottles for drinking water. 10. Distress signals. 11. First-aid kit. 12. Sleeping bags. 13. Camera and film (in watertight bags). 14. Watertight Sony video cameras. 15. Flashlights and flares. 16. Rowing seat. 17. Radar reflectors. 18. Desalination pumps (static and standby). 19, 20, 21, 22. The sea anchors, with their anchor ropes.

. . . plus everything already on board:
Six solar panels — Batteries — Two pairs of oars — Nautical maps and charts — Sextant — Radio — Telex — Hotplate — Kettle — Pot — Fishing gear — Two desalination pumps — Compass — Speed log — Ballast pump — Tools — Repair kit for hull — Three containers of wine (five liters each). *Laurent de Bartilla.*

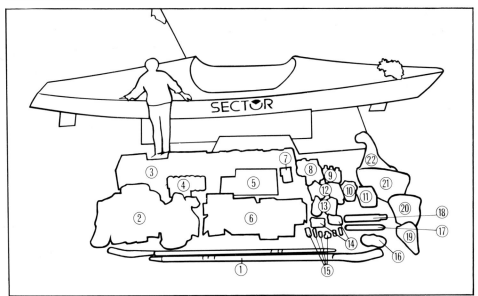

Sector as it arrived in the United States.
Photo taken from the trawler
Miss Mary.
Dominique Aubert/Sygma.

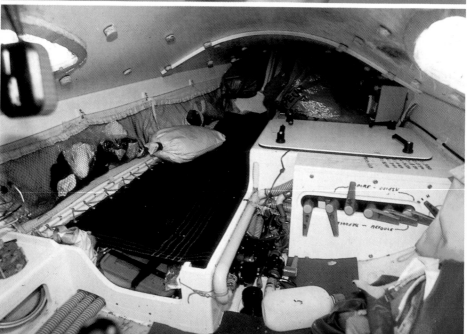

The traditional method of plotting my position — the sextant and the chronometer — enabled me to economize on batteries used in plotting by satellite. *Gerard d'Aboville/Sygma.*

A look at my watertight cabin. To the right, the series of levers that enabled me to utilize seawater to shift ballast from one tank to the other in order to right *Sector* when it capsized. Behind the ballast levers, the watertight compartment housing the radio equipment. *Dominique Aubert/Sygma.*

Twelve hours a day, seventeen strokes a minute, was my routine whenever the weather allowed. *Gerard d'Aboville/Sygma.*

If my basic chow was the packages of dehydrated food, from time to time I would spell them by opening one of Captain Cook's delectable canned goods. *Gerard d'Aboville/Sygma.*

Sector with its sea anchors out,
coping with the giant swells.
This picture was taken from the *Miss Mary* on November 19,
just a day before I landed. *Sygma.*

INSERT: September 2,
just after I was caught in the cockpit
when the boat capsized. I had the camera in my hand at the time,
and as I crawled back up on the overturned hull,
I took this picture before I set to work getting
Sector turned right-side up.
Gerard d'Aboville/Sygma.

November 19. When the trawler *Miss Mary*
came out to find me in gale force winds, it
found *Sector* with its hull to the heavens. *Sygma.*

TOP INSERT: A few hours later, a view of *Miss Mary*
in those angry seas, as seen from *Sector.*
Gerard d'Aboville/Sygma.

BOTTOM INSERT: When *Sector* capsized that last time,
there was a crack in my cabin ceiling a good fifteen centimeters
(about six inches) long. *Gerard d'Aboville/Sygma.*

When *Sector* capsized, it was not unlike being in an automobile accident: there were times when I emerged with my face a bloody mess and my body a mass of bruises. *Gerard d'Aboville/Sygma.*

Sector during one of the times it capsized, as I was pumping seawater into the lateral ballast tanks to try to right it. *Gerard d'Aboville/Sygma.*

TOP: *Sector* and me on an unusually calm sea, as seen from the Russian freighter *Pskor*, which chanced upon me on October 29 and insisted I come on board — an invitation I politely declined. *Sygma.*

BOTTOM: *Pskor* as seen from *Sector*, with, in the foreground, the French flag flying from my antenna. *Gerard d'Aboville/Sygma.*

OPPOSITE: Photo taken from the *Miss Mary* on November 20. Olivier de Kersauson, on board the *Miss Mary*, signaled to me to turn around and take a look: behind me was the American coastline. *Dominique Aubert/Sygma.*

November 21, 1215 hours: I entered the port of Ilwaco, in the state of Washington. From this moment on my crossing would be no more than a memory. Yet, as recently as the day before, I was a boxer on the ropes, and the Pacific seemed intent on taking me down for the count. This is who the passengers on the *Miss Mary* encountered when they found me out on the high seas. TOP: *Gilles Klein/Sipa Sport;* BOTTOM: *Dominique Aubert/Sygma.*

The crowds fell silent; it was the magical moment. With *Sector* still claiming me, Cornélia, Ann, and Guillaume gave in and let their tears flow. *Dominique Aubert/Sygma.*

Cornélia and Ann looking on pensively as what was left of me was examined. I had thought I had probably lost seven to ten kilos (about fifteen to twenty-two pounds) in the course of the crossing, but in fact I had lost seventeen kilos, about thirty-seven pounds. *Gerard d'Aboville Archives.*

TOP: The survivor. *Gilles Klein/Sipa Sport*

BOTTOM: Portrait of the Survivor as a Young Boy. At least there seems to be a continuity. . . . *Gerard d'Aboville Archives/Sygma.*

reflection. In my case, with entire days of rowing during which I had nothing else to do but think, the opportunity was ample. Perfect. Yet, I knew that my most profound reflections would come later, much later, when all my intimations and intuitions had been tried and tested against reality.

It would never have crossed my mind before setting out on this voyage to ask myself what such an adventure might bring in the way of insights into the meaning of life. If there were something to be discovered, I might discover it . . . and then again, I might not. Only time would tell.

At least two times I might well have given up. Two times when death seemed the easiest way out. Physical exhaustion, distress reinforced by solitude, the conviction that any future was vain — all were circumstances that "paved the way."

Why, then, did I keep on fighting tooth and nail? The survival instinct? True, but what, after all, is the instinct to survive? Was it the anguish that swept over me whenever I thought of how my family and close friends would suffer if I did give up? All of which overly complicates the question at any given moment of agony. In that instant the animal instinct takes over; the brain is entirely monopolized, the whole mind focused on coping with the immediate problem at hand, of reacting, of doing the precise thing that has to be done if one is to survive.

So what is it, then?

Only later, in full tranquility, did it occur to me that, very simply, I was not yet ready to die.

And what if life were a trajectory and death its natural conclusion in the same way that seasons succeed each other? Did you ever see a tree lose its buds or springtime leaves, except in the case of some accident of nature?

Death is doubtless only a stage, but a stage to be taken in due course, a stage that — again, except for an accident of nature — generally occurs for a human being somewhere between the ages of sixty and eighty, after a lifetime of fulfillment, during which time each of the stages has its role and place: a time to grow, a time to build and create, a time to grow old — to mention only the principle phases, each filled with its own experiences, memories, joys, and sorrows.

The anguish of dying before you see your children grow up, for instance, is one category of those "unfinished stages" — for your children, it means a broken youth; for you, the golden years cut off. These concerns are of far greater importance than any material consideration in life.

And, at the end of his or her voyage, the person who has enjoyed a full trajectory will, I feel sure, approach death with great serenity.

Does all this imply an intuition of the afterlife?

Perhaps. Do not look to me for an answer: I still have a good way to go on my voyage. In fact, if all goes well, I am only about halfway down my road of life.

8

Typhoons

September 5

Happy birthday, Gerard! I hesitate to use the word happy *because the day is beginning very badly. Winds from the southeast, with increasing velocity, barometer falling, rain, and a pitch-black sky.*

A lot to look forward to: another twenty-four hours of punishment.

Come what may, I'd at least reached the ripe old age of forty-six, which wasn't bad. Only a few days ago I wouldn't have put money on it.

Prow facing due east, with my sea anchors out, I tried to make the best of a bad situation by pausing to read the letters my family had given me before my departure, to be opened only on my birthday. I couldn't help feeling nostalgic, and tears welled up despite my efforts to force them back. In my situation, words had a very special resonance and were so much more moving than they would have been under normal conditions.

I opened Ann's present first: a lovely bar of soap in the shape of a fish whose perfume filled my watertight quarters. Then Guillaume's: a double present. First a book entitled *Tintin in America*, doubtless to help me find my way around once I arrived; then a copy of *Playboy*, with a written note on the cover reminding me that it was only on loan and that it was to be returned to the rightful owner once I was back on dry land.

The fact was, I did not have enough to read on board. A question of weight, which had obliged me to make serious cuts and omissions: a book by Henry de Montfried, another by Alphonse Allais, a third by Edgar Allen Poe. But I had kept on board my favorite, Frank Bullen's classic *The Cruise of the Cachalot,* which is the story of sailors' lives a hundred and fifty years ago on a great whaling ship. Their lot was so terrible I almost forgot my own trials and tribulations!

September 7

0430: another capsize.
0630: another capsize, this time extremely violent.

The second time *Sector* flipped over, I hit my head very hard against the bulkhead. Fortunately, I was wearing my wool cap. It was a rough day ahead with waves of twenty feet and more.

Between two waves, I dashed toward the forward part of the boat to check on the state of my foodstuffs. According to the sky and the weather reports, my problems were only just beginning.

Ensconced once more in my cabin, I began to question myself again about my future, which was a way of escaping reality.

The success or failure of the voyage was the incessant, ever-burning question. Yet I knew the answer by heart. I knew that, even if I were successful, there would be a brief moment of exaltation, when everything would be simple and easy. But life — real life — would soon reassert itself, with all its demands and banalities. I also had to face the possibility of failure: something serious might happen to the boat, or to me. That thought was the unkindest cut of all: so much pain and suffering, so much self-investment for naught. Even assuming a failure in which I survived but failed to reach my goal, wouldn't I be affected forever? Maybe not, for I would have fought the good fight to the bitter end. But whenever that comforting thought came to mind I knew immediately, in my heart of hearts, that I was letting myself off too easily. In this kind of undertaking, it was all or nothing.

When life is reduced to a struggle to survive, everything else — glory, fame, fortune — pales to insignificance. All the gold in the world, all the honors that might be heaped upon me by others, seem virtually meaningless next to the question: am I *really* going to make it?

Night of September 7/8

I was sound asleep, wrapped in a slicker in an attempt to keep myself warm despite the fact that my sleeping sack was sopping wet. Together the two pieces of equipment were combination survival gear and antishock device. Since I'd had my fill of the sound of roaring waves, I'd plugged my ears in an effort to catch up on my sleep. As a result, I heard nothing and felt nothing this time. The boat capsized on the bunkside, that is, to starboard, and I only woke up once the boat was hull up!

September 8: Repeat

I know two very unhappy kids today, namely Guillaume and Ann, since this is their first day of school. As for me, I am relatively happy: I've just crossed the international dateline — hence the "repeat." I'm going to live September 8 all over again. As if once were not enough.

Absolutely wretched weather, barometer falling, the boat off again and running. Retreat into my watertight shelter, with a knot in my stomach. Typhoon "Ivy" is heading inexorably toward the North Pacific.

When I set out on this adventure I was not unaware that late in the summer and early in the fall typhoons formed in the Pacific. Despite the many successive delays in Japan that had kept me from leaving on schedule, I was still virtually certain that I would avoid the worst of them. But I also knew that I would probably not be able to avoid them altogether and was counting on being able to skirt them.

These meteorological monsters would doubtless wipe me out in a trice if I had the misfortune of running smack into them while they were at their peak. I had a hard time imagining what it would be like to be caught in cyclonic winds of from 120 to 180 miles per hour, out on the high seas. Few are the mariners who have experienced these monsters of nature and lived to tell the tale. Although I had managed to steer clear of the centers of these low pressure "great winds,"* I felt their breath on my back. For weeks on end I would live with this menace, spawned in

* The term typhoon comes from the Chinese *tai-fung*, literally "great wind."

distant waters, that seemed to pursue me in the North Pacific. First Ivy, then Luke, followed by Mireille and Orchid. Gentle names that wrought havoc on the Asian continent, leaving hundreds of dead in their wake before pursuing their relentless course across the ocean. Some typhoons aborted, but those I cited remained powerful enough to head north in my direction, too far away to wipe me out but close enough to generate enormous waves that did affect me. On the plus side, they also sent me hurtling in an easterly direction.

Typhoons don't materialize out of nowhere, without warning. Weather stations track them from their inception, so I was always fully aware of their impending arrival. I spent a full week watching and waiting expectantly for them, readying the boat as best I could, making sure *Sector* and I were as ready as possible when D-day arrived.

By the time I saw Ivy arrive on the distant horizon, it had already claimed some two hundred lives.

September 11 and 12

Late in the afternoon, the sky turned livid. The troughs of the waves yawned like deepening canyons, and the winds ranged between gale force 6 and 7. On two occasions, I stuck my nose outside, intending to film the scene, and both times almost turned to tragedy. I cursed myself. Even if I were trying to stiffen my spine by resorting to film, I could not under any circumstances let down my guard.

Hundreds of birds overhead, fleeing the monster. Heading due south. A feeling of cataclysm. Ashen sunset, followed by a night of complete horror. Sector tossed about in every direction.

119

1800: Boat capsizes.
2320: Two capsizes, one after the other.
0120: Sector capsizes again.
This list will be too long to relate. . . .
0300: Backward somersault, all of a sudden. I'm thrown
forward. The boat makes a full somersault before return-
ing to the vertical. Then it turns back again, upside down.

Most of the times *Sector* turned over it was from a wave
that hit broadside. This time it was grabbed by a monster
wave, hurled downward, downward, faster and faster. Then
suddenly the prow hit the sea as though it had run smack
into a brick wall. I could feel the whole craft shudder, and
the massive blow on the cabin wall made me think it was
going to snap. The shock was so brutal I thought the porthole was going to explode right in my face. From one second
to the next I had gone from twenty-five knots to a full stop.
I was hurled against the bulkhead. At the same moment,
the hull moved from a forty-five degree downward angle to
completely vertical, prow skyward, before quivering and
falling backward. A descent of at least twenty-five feet.
Three full stories. The same feeling you'd have inside a car
somersaulting off a cliff.

An inventory of the damage reveals several cracks in the
inner lining of the hull, as well as in the door and cabin
deck.
As for myself, two broken ribs, a nose that's turned into
a shapeless, swollen mass. Nervous exhaustion. Physi-
cally, a basket case.

During my Atlantic crossing, I did not have a life raft with
me nor even a distress signal such as I had on board *Sector*.
I did not even have a life jacket, and yet I can honestly say

that never have I have been as frightened as I was during my hours battling to survive Ivy. The Pacific is so different from the Atlantic, so much harsher and unforgiving. Not that I have not had my share of close calls. I remember once when I was sailing along the Brittany coast some fifteen years ago, in charge of a convoy of sailing ships. Cornélia was with me, as was Guillaume — then two months old — and two other people. It was night, and all of a sudden, out of nowhere, came this great gust of wind that sank the ship. Just like that. We all managed to make it to the life raft, but it wasn't long before that went down, too, leaving us in the high seas in mid-November. I saw myself dying, and my family with me. As luck would have it, one of the sailing vessels I was escorting saw us and, just in time, fished us out of the water.

Now even that experience paled before the gnawing, nagging, burning, subterranean fear that for weeks had held me in its grip.

I confess, without the slightest bit of shame, that fear is by now part and parcel of my being. It follows me like a shadow, always present, latent during the rare hours of relative calm, carrying on its patient task of undermining my morale, forever ready to move in during difficult times, ready to strike at the slightest sign of letdown.

If fear is inevitable, it is nonetheless ignoble. Demeaning. It does not station itself in the head or heart, as other emotions do, but in the belly. To face fear and overcome it is a source of great pride and satisfaction. It is the greatest victory, that of the mind over the animal. An illusory refutation of the human condition? Perhaps. The sin of haughtiness or legitimate pride? We all have to judge for ourselves.

Risk is not an end in itself — to play the role of daredevil by hanging on to the tail of an airplane or going over Niagara Falls in a barrel, no thanks! Yet for me risk — real risk — is the salt of life. It accompanies and flatters my penchant for daring solutions, for panache, for the "heroic" and gratuitous act. I think of risk as one of the indispensable ingredients that validates victory and makes it taste so sweet.

We often speak of calculated risks. I don't quite know what that expression includes. If it means smothering risk beneath a plethora of precautions, nothing is left. By comparison, the lucid appreciation of danger, to which one adds solid experience, careful preparation, and material adapted to the situation you plan to confront, simply gives you a better chance at success, enables you to raise the stakes further, to expand the limits.

I have always had a great need for personal freedom. Other people sometimes think that I'm not interested in them because I treat them the way I would like to be treated; that is, I totally respect their privacy — and that includes their thoughts, opinions, and feelings. It is very possible that I carry this so-called virtue too far. But the fact is, I never intrude on other people's privacy unless they specifically ask me to. Maybe this tendency is sometimes misconstrued as a lack of interest on my part. But I confess that I have never understood why I should be obliged to ask people every morning how their cat or canary is doing today, as if I really cared. By the same token, I ask others to leave me alone, to tend my garden any way I see fit.

I know, too, that my desire for independence and autonomy — which, I admit, I carry fairly far — does not fit in very well with certain widespread values in our overly civilized society: social security, life insurance, all the other kinds of insurance designed to protect us from the risks of the world, not to mention a whole slew of other codes and regulations. I fully understand the need for a driver to have automobile insurance, as I understand that one should respect the basic rules of the road. But the bewildering increase in the rules that govern our lives strikes me as more than a little stultifying.

When I say that I value my personal freedom above all else, I also accept the other side of that coin, namely that I take full responsibility for my actions and conduct. Not ninety or ninety-five percent, but one hundred percent. This voyage across the North Pacific is, to my mind, the supreme responsibility, because in putting my life on the line I have risked my all.

True responsibility, the ultimate exercise of one's freedom, is to know that in the event you fail you expose yourself to the supreme penalty, death. That in itself is enough to make me feel the full weight of what I do. All the rest is so much literature.

I have chosen the ocean as my field of confrontation or, if you will, my field of battle. Because the ocean is reality at its toughest and most demanding. As my weapons against this awesome power, I have human values: intelligence, experience, and the stubborn will to win.

9

Indelibly Inscribed

September 13

Today is Friday the 13th! I haven't forgotten you, Princess. You can pick whatever restaurant you want, and I'll take you there as soon as I get back.

One day Ann, who was born on Friday the 13th, came home from school in tears. The kids had made fun of her for having such a terrible birthday. "Didn't you know," they said, "that Friday the 13th brings bad luck?" To prove them wrong, I always invited Ann, on this presumably fateful day, to the restaurant of her choice. At first I kept things pretty much under control, since my little Princess was crazy about hamburgers. But it wasn't long before she caught on, and recently she's been making noises about the Tour d'Argent, which, if it isn't Paris's most expensive restaurant, comes pretty close. So much for my low-cost crusade against superstition!

Speaking of superstition, my teakettle occupied a very special spot on my stove and was held in place with an elastic cord in case the boat overturned. Often when I'd put back the kettle, the handle struck the edge of the table and made a sound like a note on the scale. I'd always put out a finger to stop it, a reflex that came down to me from my mother. When we were growing up, whenever Mother would set a metal plate down on the table — or any kind of metal platter for that matter — she would always interrupt the sound by murmuring, "A sailor's drowning." I presume that in her mind the sailor would have drowned had she not intervened with her magic phrase. Over the course of many years, I also have to believe that she has saved from certain death the equivalent of the crew of an aircraft carrier.

As for myself, I'm not superstitious. But you never know . . . I remember that at the headquarters of Lloyd's of London there is a bell that rings in memory of those who have lost their lives at sea. Considering my present situation, one can never be too careful.

I discovered that my solar panels, which doubtless had been submerged too long because of the number of times *Sector* had capsized, had ceased functioning. A catastrophe. From a morale viewpoint, it was a veritable disaster to have lost contact with the outside world. From a purely practical viewpoint, losing contact with FK8CR meant that I would no longer be able to track the weather. The worst was, the last time I had heard from FK8CR, it was to learn that another typhoon was heading my way.

I took advantage of a moment of relative calm to try to repair the solar panels. Normally there's nothing you can do to restart them once they've shut down. The metal contacts were ruined, completely eroded by the humidity. But I had no choice. I started first with the starboard panels, which had been less exposed to the sea than the portside panels. First I had to take them apart, fiddle with the joints using a copper wire, and, because I had nothing else on board to make the panels watertight again, smother the whole thing with epoxy, which takes hours to dry. To speed up the drying process, I heated up my magic potion in a spoon by holding it over one of my camp stove burners, then rushed outside to apply it. I made several such round trips, covering my repairs with a product that forms a yellowish crust as it dries. Poor Bernard! When I think of all the trouble he went to building *Sector*, making sure the hull and deck were immaculate, and now the whole deck area was a mess, splattered with spots of dried glue! But my mad efforts did bear fruit: one after another the solar panels began to emerge from their deep slumber. Not only did they emerge: soon they were functioning again at a hundred percent capacity!

September 14

0800: Sector *capsizes once again, but this time gently. Another ridiculous day, with the westerly winds pushing me back in the wrong direction.*

Every two or three hours I opened the cabin to let in some air. This morning I spent five full hours cooped up inside, until I began having trouble breathing. Even my cigarette lighter wouldn't light because of the lack of oxygen. I kept wondering just how long one could remain holed up in the cabin without fainting. I only hoped that before losing consciousness I would somehow be jolted awake. What a great feeling it was whenever I opened the cabin door, especially after the low oxygen had begun to make me drowsy. I was like someone who had not had a drop of water for days and was immersed in a lake of clear blue water. I filled my lungs with air, breathing in deeply again and again, almost giddy.

I have been totaling up the number of times I have cap-sized. The results are hardly encouraging.

I've turned over nineteen times to date, which is bad enough. But it's the progression that is alarming:
- *once in July*
- *four times in August*
- *already fourteen times so far in September*

In other words, an average of once a day this month! How long can I hold out? Or, more to the point, how many more times will I be able to right Sector without something going wrong? Because it's not as though the more times I go through it the better I get. On the contrary. Each time it happens the effect is cumulative, stretching my nerves ever tighter. I know that in any event I'll come out of this — assuming I do — marked for life.

Before I set out I trained physically, not unlike a boxer preparing for a bout. Not by making any wild statements, not by declaring to the world that my opponent was worth-less and my intention was to knock him out in the early rounds. No, the Pacific is not an opponent you knock out. You have to be prepared to go the full fifteen rounds and hope for a decision.

But at this point in the bout I felt like a boxer who no longer had the strength to fight back, because he was at the point of utter exhaustion. So all he could do was hang in there, protect himself by keeping his guard up, keep on the defensive, bob and weave. To make any headway, I had to fight against myself, against the nagging desire to throw in the sponge. Short of that, all I could do was parry the blows thrown at me, avoiding them as best I could, and when I couldn't, simply take them. Two other handicaps: loneliness and duration, that is, the endless, ever-slowing

127

passage of time. With these two elements dogging me, the dice were really loaded.

September 21

Typhoon Luke had made its presence felt. As I was using the sextant to chart my position, just outside the cabin door, I was almost swept overboard by a giant wave. Even if my safety harness had saved me, the notion that the boat would have capsized with the cabin door open sent chills up my spine.

I looked back at my log for the day and found noted there: *For God's sake, be more careful!*

In bad weather — that is, more and more frequently — my every movement and gesture had to be thought out in advance, examined, and reflected on; strict rules had to be meticulously followed. Acting on the realistic principle that *Sector* could capsize at any moment, I knew that I would have time only to make one, almost reflexive, movement and maybe not even that. To take just one example, in preparing my dehydrated food I always had to close the porthole before I lit the burner. Then I had to keep my finger on the gas button while the water was heating, so that at the slightest alert I could turn off the flame. As soon as the water was boiling, I put back the stove, then aired out the cabin briefly, for at this point it would be completely steamed up. Then back to the kettle, whose boiling contents always presented a considerable danger. Sometimes it took me a full fifteen minutes just to prepare a cup of coffee.

By now I had become maniacal when it came to being

neat. Everything on board was so perfectly in order that I could have lived in my cabin with my eyes closed without any problem. Tirelessly, I would sponge the ceiling to wipe off the condensation that had accumulated, or I would sponge the bottom of the boat, to reduce the amount of water that would inevitably gather there as well. The constant dampness in the cabin made living there almost unbearable.

Today I learned via radio from Christopher that Frédéric Guérin, who had set out to break my record for rowing across the Atlantic, had given up, becalmed off the coast of Ireland. He had fallen increasingly behind my own schedule, and as the gap increased he must have decided there was no hope of ever catching up. Had he had his share of bad luck, including, I suspected, not being able to take full advantage of the Gulf Stream? It was true that in 1980 I had benefited from a summer during which there had been an unusual number of low pressure systems.

By the time Guérin gave up, his radio was on the blink. The news depressed me, for I had been following his progress from the Pacific with great interest. Now, with him gone, I felt even more alone than ever.

September 22

I realized that I was only halfway across. For a long time I had been looking forward to this day as a time of celebration, a moment of great accomplishment. Now that I had reached it, I actually felt depressed. I had the sense that I had already been out here for a lifetime, and the notion that I was only halfway there, that the stretch ahead was as long as the one behind, struck me as beyond both my ability and my strength.

Starting then, I decided that not only would I cross off the days on the little calendar at the back of my log as they occurred in the future, but I would go back and furiously cross off the days in the past, one at a time. This was a curious attempt to wipe them out, to forget them completely, as though they had never occurred.

Because this was a red-letter day, I couldn't help mentally calculating how long it was going to take me from here on out. If the second half of the trip took as long as the first, then I should reach the American coast on December 5. But if I subtracted the fourteen days in August when headwinds had kept me from making any progress at all, then I ought to be there on November 21. I did my best to convince myself that the earlier date was the realistic one, but even that seemed so far off. Besides, I knew that October and November were much more difficult months than July and August. Could I really hold out?

Meanwhile, back to the grind. I took up my oars again and rowed, rowed, rowed. . . .

September 23

For the first time I managed to make contact with an American radio-communication station, KMI. For weeks I had been trying to contact the station, without success, so I took this to be a major breakthrough. In any case, it was tangible proof of progress. What was more, it meant that I would henceforth be able to contact my family, via KMI, by telephone. The only problem was, the KMI technician informed me, that in order to put my call through I would have to set up an account with the station. How in the world did he expect me to set out up an account when I was still thousands of miles away? In trying to explain my situation, I lost many precious amp-hours of electricity. I persisted. I ranted and raved. All I got in return was: "I'm sorry. I'm really sorry!" In the end I was so upset that I burst into tears. I was furious at the whole world. What in the hell was Christopher *doing* back in Paris?

Fortunately, I was still in regular contact with Eddy, which enabled me to pass on the information about my billing problem with KMI and ask if he could help me out, way over there on the other side of the world. He was only too happy to oblige.

Speaking of Eddy, I had never set eyes on him, yet his voice was as familiar to me as those of my family and closest friends. I would search for him on the wavelengths, and even when the static was at its worst and I could barely hear a thing, I would always immediately recognize his voice.

In the course of our conversations, I discovered little by little what his life was like and conjured up in my mind both what he looked like and what kind of person he was. I realized, too, that he was now spending much more of his leisure time collecting weather data specifically for me, and that our radio rendezvous were taking place at hours of the day that must have been impossible for him.

The mere sound of his voice had become for me even more precious than the information he was passing on. I tried to tell him as much, but the words just wouldn't come out right, and I wasn't sure he ever got the message. If not, I hope he does when he reads this book.

September 26

Sector capsizes not once but twice. Always the same scenario, but more and more violent.

I continued to have nightmares. Last night it was the bulkhead of the cabin cracking. That was my constant terror, for *Sector*'s hull, as indicated, only maintained its rigidity thanks to two thin layers of carbon that held the foam tight. The first time it cracked, this composite material would become as fragile as an eggshell with a slight crack in it.

From then on, I slept with my distress signal beneath my head, on the bunk, fearing I would awake some night to find the cabin filled with water and the boat in pieces. As the voyage wore on, that distress signal moved increasingly closer to me, until it had become my pillow, always immediately at the ready. It was a defense mechanism on my part, but I also knew, whenever I really thought about it, that it was a fairly useless means of protection. What in the world would I do with a distress signal as I clung to one of the pieces of the boat? Assuming I did manage to send off the signal, by the time any passing ship had responded and come looking for me, I would have long since slipped into my watery grave.

September 27

Typhoon Mireille heading my way, to the north of me and moving east.

To the west, extremely heavy seas. Yet the typhoon got no closer than 600 miles from my present position. I could imagine the havoc the storm must have wrought for anything directly in its path. Here the waves were very long

132

and well over thirty feet high — great moving hills, the sure sign of a distant storm, a furious one.

For the last several days I had been intrigued by the flight of the birds overhead. No longer were their movements irregular, first going in one direction then another. Now they all seemed to be flying in the same direction — south. At first the phenomenon was barely perceptible, but today it was much more marked.

At first I'd thought the birds were simply heading away from the storm to the north, but now I had to face the irrefutable evidence: what I was seeing was their autumnal migration. They were flying south by the hundreds toward the trade winds, fleeing these latitudes that would shortly become infernal.

And then they were gone, these final companions. A dark sky, short days. Summer was gone.

October 2

I am approaching 160 degrees longitude east, and my arrival lies at 140 degrees longitude. My next objective: 155 degrees 30 minutes, at which point I will have covered two thirds of my route, a threshhold I look forward to with great anticipation.

At night I did my best to protect myself from the encroaching cold. I slept with all my clothes on, wrapped in my slicker inside my drenched sleeping bag. After a while my body warmed up, that is, everything except my feet, which were always frozen. The period just before daybreak was especially bad. Even when the weather was good enough, I found it impossible to sleep.

October 3

Around 0800, Sector *hits a wave prow first and flips over, with the porthole open.*

By some miracle, I was able to shut the porthole immediately. I had my hand on it when the wave struck. By now *Sector* had become an extension of myself; I had developed a sixth sense about it, sensing exactly what the next minute, even the next second, would bring.

Lord, but the weeks were long and painful to endure! The moon had reappeared, and I took advantage of it to row during the night; the days were now so short.

Rowing smoothly, steadily, like a robot, the body works in a banal, monotonous, stupid effort. A body that the mind has deserted. No longer any need for the mind. It was off somewhere else, doing its own thing. . . .

It was incredible how much I found myself dwelling on those days back on dry land that had passed me by and how much I regretted having missed them. First the spring, of which I had seen nothing because I had been so focused on getting *Sector* ready for the trip. I should have stocked up on all the springtime buds, all those first fragile leaves that unfurl on the trees. Then there was the summer, which this voyage had stolen from me, a summer, I was sure, that had to be the most beautiful one since God created earth, a summer filled with the sound of the crickets on the darkening air and the smell of new-mown hay, the fullness of nature that, having reached its peak, takes a momentary rest before the solstice. And now this voyage was stealing autumn from me, too: autumn with its wisps of fog lying low over the lakes and ponds, with its odor of apples and fires in the fireplace.

I was famished for tastes, for colors, for odors. Especially odors, which evoke, better than any other trigger mechanism, reminiscences of a particular place. As I rowed I hummed various songs to myself. There was Dutronc's song about the urban garden, with its wonderful ozone deep down beneath the ground, in other words, the Metro. Yes, even the smell of Paris, that mixture of dust and electricity that floats over the subway platforms, was a source of nostalgia. I also hummed country-and-western songs over and over again, where I knew the tunes but not the words, hummed them obsessively. One obsessed me especially, and I hummed it for months, without ever knowing either the words or the title. Only later did I learn that it was Alan Jackson's "Here in the Real World."

Other, more ancient songs also filled my head, such as those we sang aboard the *Lady Maud*, songs filled with a mixture of oakum, coal tar, and varnish.

This morning, no stomach even for breakfast. Utter weariness. I was dreaming of a cup of coffee and a croissant on the quiet, sun-drenched terrace of a bistro. I saw myself sitting there, reading my paper in the warm sun, watching the world go by. Everything I had never found the time to do in life now struck me as the epitome of happiness. Simply to know that that terrace existed, that it was awaiting me, even if it was a possibility I would never take advantage of, even if it was nothing but a mirage, was enough to fill me with happiness.

I told myself that when I got back, in the not too distant future, I would regale myself and my senses, that I would

135

fill my eyes and ears with sights and sounds, would fill my lungs with air, would touch and taste till I had had my fill. But I knew I could never get enough, and the detailed list of all the senses' satisfactions crowded my head.

Then I was overwhelmed with a desire to go to a village, a little village far inland where you can't see the sea, where people didn't even know the sea existed. I told myself I would make sure never to tell them about it!

A message from my brother Norbert revealed to what degree my family and close friends, in their desire to send me comfort and reassurance, had no clue, no notion, of what I was feeling. Departing from my customary reserve, I sent off a long telex in which I tried to clarify things.

DABOVIL 63L234F
SINGAPORE TELECOM
REFERENCE NO. 081083

Kindly forward to Norbert d'Aboville, who "would like to make sure I have a modicum of pleasure during my voyage."

Dear Norbert,
    There I was, yesterday morning, at the end of a perfect night. Perfect weather, almost a full moon, clear sky, a few stars that seemed to be resisting the lunar incandescence. The mild breeze gently propelling the boat forward almost made me forget I was rowing. I was thinking about your message, asking me whether I had achieved a sense of being "on top of things now."
    At the risk of disappointing you, I have to say that there is no way for me ever to feel on top of things.

The problem is, every minute, every second, all I can think about is making it, getting there, achieving my goal. My mind focuses — far too lucidly, I might add — on all the risks that stand in my way, all the obstacles that threaten to wipe out in a moment the extraordinary amount of time and effort and personal sacrifice I have put into this undertaking. I am affected, indelibly affected, by what I have just been through. While it is said that with the passage of time the most painful memories have a way of turning into positive memories, these will never change; they were, and will always remain, terrible and terrifying.

I'll never forget the many times the boat capsized, especially the one when it turned a complete somersault, throwing me against the bulkhead. Then, with my frayed nerves stretched to the breaking point, I kept waiting for the final blow, the blow that would end it all, and let out a primal scream, like some wild beast. Nor will I ever forget those other times when I battled for my life, feeling my strength waning minute by minute. And the taste of seawater in my mouth, in my lungs. The taste of death. And all that alone, alone, alone.

So in order to find a few moments of relative pleasure such as that night I just described, my only recourse is to get away from this boat, from this crossing, from this ocean. I try to tell myself that I am somewhere else, that I am walking in the desert, without any set goal, preferably without any goal at all; or else I imagine myself at the rudder of some other boat, on some other sea.

But the illusion is brief, and you have to watch out for its counterpart, the danger of letting go and feeling sorry for yourself or your situation, for if I were to let that feeling in, even for a moment, it would be like opening the gates of the fortress to your worst enemy. So I only allow myself rare moments when I picture myself elsewhere, in some wonderful never-never land, because the awakening is not only rude but dangerous.

So you think there will be an arrival? You believe it's really going to happen?

Ah, that arrival, so dreamed of, so longed for. True, the joy will be commensurate with the expectation, but also what a terrible feeling of "I've already been there." You want your happiness not to end, you want to set a little aside for tomorrow and the day after, but there's no way you can; it's the liqueur of absolute happiness, but all you have is a drop, one tiny drop, the effect of which is immediate. You see this happiness in the full knowledge that, by the very act of experiencing it, it has already been lived, it belongs to the past, and that each of these marvelous moments is already no more than a memory, as though there were no present between this future so long and so ardently awaited that I am living through now — and will live through until I get there — and the past, which will be the rest of my life after I do arrive . . . And you are there, looking at the crowd. They think it's the beginning of something. But you know it's already over.

So is there an "after"?

After — that is, after the successful completion of your daring adventure — there is a whirlwind, a touch of glory or what passes for glory, which does not last long (right after your act, don't forget the clowns come on). There is even relative material comfort. Vanity and self-interest, these pleasures are base; they inevitably enter into the calculations.

Let's talk only about the satisfactions.

So what remains?
Nothing, that's what. And that's life. Provided it lasts.

GERARD, ON BOARD SECTOR.
LATITUDE 41 DEGREES 18 MINUTES NORTH
LONGITUDE 159 DEGREES, 31 DEGREES WEST.

October 6

During the night, the wind veers suddenly to the west, the waves turn choppy. Giant sprays of white foam on either side of the cockpit.

A new kind of somersault: a complete back flip. I find myself flattened on the ceiling of the cabin, then bounced back onto my bunk.

10

Do You See the Coastline?

October 9

Via KMI, the American station that had finally consented to let me utilize its wavelengths, I was able to call my family. What a feeling of euphoria to make contact at last. After each call, my rowing day sped by so much more quickly, my head filled with a thousand little things to ponder. And their letters, which reached me now via satellite, could be read and reread as many times as I liked, giving me the impression at least that my loved ones were not all that far away. They forced me to keep thinking: what time is it for them now? What are they doing? What's the weather like over there?

Cold, but the conditions are fine, with the winds from the west at about fifteen knots. Obsessed by my goal of reaching the three-quarter mark in the crossing. Each time I attain one of these goals, however, all I can think about is not what has been accomplished but how far I still have to go.

During the evening, a ship passed by, but I wasn't able to make contact with it. Too bad. I wouldn't have minded if one of the crew had tossed a bottle of Scotch in my direction!

October 12

Yesterday evening, just as the sun was going down, the sky turned the color of polished cotton.

0500: Sector capsizes, as usual, then again at 0600. Violently both times, tossing me about in the cabin like a rag doll. Black and blue marks everywhere. My hand injured, too.

October 14

One of the little joys of the crossing: yesterday I repaired a pipe that was leaking in our Paris apartment. How? Via radio. Cornélia was on the other end of the line, and I told her which tools to use, then took her through the repair process step by step. This minor but all-important incident made me feel that I was back in contact with the real world.

It took little to entertain me these days. Running through the scene over and over again, I managed to lift my spirits and completely forgot the slave labor I was performing in the cockpit.

October 15

I decided to give myself a few hours off, and instead of getting up at daybreak and heading for the cockpit, I kept to my bunk, hoping time would move more quickly. Every once in a while a big wave would arouse me from my torpor. But after a few hours of presumed rest, I realized that the constant battering of the boat by the waves left me more tired than I had been when I had begun. As I was pulling myself out of the sleeping bag, there was something about the sound of an oncoming wave I didn't like, and I rushed to the porthole and slammed it shut. Lucky premonition — *Sector* was again on its back. Reflexes, well-practiced movements: the sleeping bag goes into its watertight cover, maneuver the ballast tanks, pump working. Even so, some water did get in before the porthole was secured, and my clothes, as well as the sleeping bag, were soaking wet.

Checking, I noted the visible decline of my physical abilities. At the start of the trip, I could produce a liter of fresh water using the desalination pump in exactly twelve minutes. This morning it took me twenty. That translated into a "decline" of over fifty percent.

Despite that, I decided that today I was going to "sacrifice" five liters of fresh water to wash down my sleeping bags, which were so impregnated with salt that they never dried. In fact, I had baptized them, respectively, the "Salt Mine" and the "Salt Marsh."

I spread both sleeping bags out to dry in the cockpit and, as if to smile on me, the sun made an appearance right on schedule to help dry them out. What a delight it would be to sleep in a clean, dry sleeping bag, without having to don a slicker! To make myself worthy of such unmitigated pleasure, and since the weather was good, I decided to put in a few nocturnal hours at the oars.

Now the nights are as long as the days. How far still to go? How far? I would give a great deal to know the answer to that question.

In five days the Paris Boat Show would open. I had wanted to reach land in time to fly there and show off *Sector*.

Again in an effort to escape reality, to turn my thoughts from the present and the burning question of survival, I focused my mind on that nautical event seven thousand miles to the east. I pictured the people there, the vast panoply of boats from all over the world, then focused on my own stand. Actually, now that I thought about it, why shouldn't we put the *Captain Cook* on display as well? Yes, I would have to mention that to Christopher.

October 17

Page 100 of my logbook, marking the hundredth day of the crossing. Last night was superb. I rowed until dawn.

I was beginning to grow weary of my dehydrated food. I hadn't taken enough sweets on board. I should have brought more chocolate, more whisky.

October 18

At dawn, wind from the south. Huge swells, and very choppy seas. Laborious route to the northeast. Heading directly toward Vancouver — or Anchorage. If this keeps up, I'll wind up in Alaska. Hellishly hard. Soaking wet from head to foot. I stop rowing, totally depressed. I hurt all over. Progress report: ten lousy knots. Morale at its lowest ebb.

Contrary to what some people may think, there is nothing masochistic about a crossing such as mine. Masochism consists of inflicting pain on oneself in order to derive pleasure from it. In my own case, I do concoct difficult situations but only in order to derive pleasure afterward, once the victory has been won. It is true that the more perils there are, the greater the satisfaction at having overcome them. I will have climbed a tall mountain, and earned my own esteem. But pain for pain's sake has never held any attraction for me whatsoever.

We all have the desire — overt or covert — to accomplish some very difficult task, something that will instill pride in ourselves. Anyone who thinks that a suicidal tendency is an element of the picture is totally wrong. If I had ever had the slightest tendency in that direction, I would have been dead long ago. It's not as though there were lack of opportunities. It is, rather, the opposite tendency at work here, namely the insatiable will to survive. In the course of this crossing, my survival instinct was ten times, a hundred times, a thousand times, stronger than it is in the course of a so-called normal life, because I want with all my heart and soul to reach my goal.

I have not been conditioned or programmed by any techniques of auto-suggestion. I have programmed myself, focused ever since the project began on a single objective: get there, reach my goal.

I also add an element of pugnaciousness. Not aggressiveness, which I think is the wrong word. But pugnaciousness, which I think is what it's all about. A combative spirit. Without it, I don't think there's a prayer in hell you could ever see it through to the bitter end.

Completely demoralized, I'm beginning to have a very serious sense of failure. What I need, and need badly, is

144

a series of low pressure systems, bringing me winds out of the west, and I am getting nothing of the sort. Worse, according to Eddy, there are no low pressure systems anywhere on the horizon.

Winter was not far off, with everything that implies, starting with increasingly cold weather. Since I was in the midst of high pressure systems, I was shrouded in fog, which meant that my solar panels were no longer charging. My telex was permanently on the blink.

In the evening, to add insult to injury, the moon appeared from behind the clouds — an almost full moon — just as the sun was so low on the horizon that it could do nothing to help my solar panels.

October 22

The wind had fallen, and I was rowing under the full moon. I much preferred the moon — a heavenly body you could gaze upon — to the blinding sun. And besides, on moonlit nights I got the impression I was making far faster progress than I could make by day.

October 27

I crossed the thousand-mile mark, that is, the point that was only a thousand miles from shore. The last thousand miles. Winds light out of the southwest, and I was moving right along the forty-fourth parallel, at the rate of about a degree of longitude per day. Twelve days had passed without *Sector* capsizing. Quite an exploit! My obsession to get there, to reach land, was getting out of hand; it was so overwhelming that it kept waking me up in the middle of the night. I sent Christopher my projected ETAs, giving him my most optimistic and pessimistic dates. It would be between November 21 and December 1. The 21st: my God, that was only a little more than three weeks away!

October 28

Ring around the moon, a bad sign.

October 29

Strange how I had developed an acute sixth sense, a gift of double vision. Was it perhaps because I had so much time for reflection and analysis? Or was it possibly that my mind was so much more receptive? Rid of the normal intrusions of daily life, could my mind have enlarged and become more perceptive?

There were times, for example, when for no reason at all I would be thinking of a friend whom I hadn't seen in years, and when I talked to Christopher I was not at all surprised to hear him say that that very person had just called the office. The most astonishing aspect of the phenomenon was that it struck me as perfectly commonplace and normal.

In any case, this morning I had the distinct feeling that today would be marked by an encounter. Not only did I have an intuition that I was going to make contact with a ship, but I knew that it would be a very specific contact. I was so sure, in fact, that when a freighter hoved into view on the horizon, I already had my camera, my video, and my VHF radio right next to me, and the French flag was flying from the radio antenna!

It was the Russian freighter *Pskov*, out of Vladivostok, headed for Vancouver. Against all odds, but precisely as I had intuited, the ship reversed engines and came to a complete halt, to allow me to pull alongside.

"What are you doing here?" the captain asked.

"I'm going to the United States."

"So are we. Come on board."

Convinced that I was dying to join them, they unfurled a rope ladder down the side. They were completely taken aback when I politely declined. They assumed I had just arrived from outer space.

The crew took pictures. When they arrived in Vancouver, they were surprised to be greeted by a reception committee: Christopher, whom I alerted in Paris via radio, had arranged to have the ship met, so that the photos could be couriered back to France, where they appeared the following week on the cover of a weekly news magazine.

Another happy anniversary: I had crossed another time zone and was now on Pacific Standard Time.

October 31

A stroke of bad luck. Yesterday I lost the larger of my two sea anchors, its rope frayed from its swivel.

It was a serious blow. More serious than I wanted to admit. Now I could no longer prevent the southerly storms from pushing me inexorably northward. Without my sea anchor, my chances of putting in to San Francisco were virtually nil.

147

That was a disappointment but nothing compared to the realization that, to the north, the American coast was very inhospitable and the seas, at this time of year, extremely rough.

My appetite was steadily decreasing. I was eating only one meal a day. My growing lassitude regarding the dehydrated food was augmented by not being able to keep myself from conjuring up images of juicy steaks and bright green salads. I had the feeling I had lost a fair amount of weight, but with my many layers of clothing I couldn't swear to it. My guess was that I had lost somewhere between fifteen and twenty pounds, which was about what I'd lost during my Atlantic crossing.

After dark, a shower of shooting stars streaked across the sky, one of them lighting up the heavens like a bolt of lightning.

November 1

The south wind continues unabated. A horrible night, with the stern of the boat striking the water every two hours like a cannon shot. The foulest weather imaginable. Driving rain. Thunderous noise.

I was sequestered in my cabin, writing the above by candlelight, since there was no more electricity. Battered by the storm. Winter had set in, and I felt like tossing in the towel. The thought of all those cheering me on, who wanted me to succeed, helped me to hang on.

November 3

Completely out of "hooch," a homemade eau-de-vie my father had given me to take on the trip, I'm reduced to using the rubbing alcohol from my first-aid kit. I needed a little pick-me-up to restore my flagging spirits and poured some alcohol in my coffee. Frankly, the brew was undrinkable, but what the hell.

If the definition of an alcoholic is somebody who imbibes excessive quantities of alcohol, then I'm not an alcoholic. But I was nonetheless beginning to ask myself the question. Directly behind my number one desire — or, more properly, obsession — to make landfall in America, was my craving for a good glass of wine in a real glass; or a gin and tonic, a Scotch, a martini. But above all I craved the glass of good wine. And if in fact I was a closet alcoholic, and I set off on this adventure without weighing fully all the consequences of that possibility (I had only one five-liter jug of wine left, which I did not dare open), then all these weeks of forced abstinence should have served as an almost certain cure. But abstinence had the opposite effect. The longer I remained on the wagon, the more I dreamed about drinking. From that I concluded I was incurable. To make matters worse, my memories seized on various occasions when I had drunk this or that memorable wine, and I relived those glorious moments in living color. No alcoholic memory escaped the widening net of my memories. Ah yes, that cool bottle of beer we savored in the British port of Falmouth — the only beer in the house, but did it taste good! And what about that divine bottle of Bordeaux that the former owner of the *Lady Maud* had given us, that English millionaire we just happened to meet when we put into port at Bénodet in December of 1972. Oh, and that suspect bottle of Burgundy we drank in Beaune that day in 1981. And that whisky, that delicious whisky and soda we had on the deck of *Lady Maud* in the bay of Bantry twenty years ago. Then on to the Place de l'Ecole Militaire in Paris where, on the terrace of a bistro, we savored a wonderful dark beer. . . .

I seemed to remember virtually every drink of note I'd ever had, and quite a few of little note. Not only the drinks themselves but the shape of the glasses, the color of the liquid, the reflections of glass and bottle on the table, the atmosphere of each and every setting, and, of course, the taste, the exquisite taste. My memory went so far as to transport me back to my earliest discoveries in this area, back to the family house in Kérantré, where as a wayward child I used to sneak sips of Cointreau and Benedictine, alone and in hiding from prying eyes but surrounded by the disapproving stares of the family ancestors who gazed down at me severely from their appointed places on the library walls. Foremost among them, the General seemed to disapprove most heartily.

One day, having indulged a bit more than usual, having used as my source of supply my grandmother's homemade black currant brandy, which she prized above all others, I was dozing in one of the easychairs when, in my stupor, I heard her voice behind me, growling, "Bad boy! Sure as I'm your grandmother, you'll end up an alcoholic!"

November 4

Gusting winds. Heavy swells.

In the morning, as I was talking to Christopher on the phone, I realized that at this point we were not only geographically worlds apart but worlds apart in our thinking. The subject under discussion was plane reservations, and for him it was a matter of utmost importance. He wanted to make sure he booked tickets for all those who wanted to be in the States when I arrived. Arrived? The thought still seemed so far off to me. Christopher was living in "Parisian time" while my time was slowness and perseverance. To pin things down, he wanted to know exactly when and where I planned to land. I blew my stack, not realizing that to secure thirty or forty plane tickets for a single flight was not a given, or at least could not be accomplished overnight. But what could I tell him? I now knew that the chances of making landfall in San Francisco were slight, as I also knew that the final stage of my journey would be difficult and painful.

Now I was doing everything in my power to keep *Sector* headed for San Francisco, because that was the place I had picked to land, whereas the real goal of the voyage had been simply to make landfall somewhere in North America. At this point I was 500 miles from Vancouver Island and a good 800 from San Francisco. It would be ridiculous on my part to keep focusing on a secondary objective — San Francisco — that was increasingly inaccessible, especially since I had lost the larger of my two anchors. The problem was, I was approaching a rugged coast, one of the most dangerous in the world, where ports are few and far between. To make matters worse, these ports are generally protected by barrier reefs that are impossible to cross in bad weather. The central issue was to bring *Sector* ashore safely — and me with it — rather than organizing some wonderful ceremony.

Night was now fourteen hours long, and yet I slept less and less, completely obsessed by the desire to reach shore.

November 7

Everything I thought or did was merely a pretense for figuring out where I was in relation to my arrival. I had seventeen cigarettes left; I would smoke one a day, hoping that I would have enough to last me till I landed. I took out a tank of bottled gas, telling myself that it was certain to be the last, or next to last. Well, maybe two more. The one thing I refused to do was count the strokes of my oars; that would have been sheer torture.

Memories, memories . . . In September 1980, on the train that was bringing a friend to the Brittany port of Brest as part of the welcoming committee to celebrate the triumphant conclusion of my Atlantic crossing, the friend turned to a journalist sitting next to him and said, "From what I just heard on the radio, apparently Gerard's hands have doubled in size."

The next day newspaper headlines blared: HIS HANDS ARE TWICE THEIR SIZE! As soon as I landed, everyone rushed to see what my hands looked like. Their comments were varied, but this one made me chuckle for a long time afterward: "God, his hands must have really been tiny when he started!"

It took them a long time to realize that my hands were just like anyone else's. But the initial impression is always what counts. A decade later, scarcely a week went by without somebody stopping me to say:

"I still remember those hands of yours, poor fellow, when you pulled in at Brest. They were twice their normal size!"

*　　*　　*

At Choshi, before I departed, a Japanese journalist insisted on taking a photograph of my hands. What he should have photographed were my buttocks. That's the part of my anatomy that suffered most during the crossing.

As for my hands, they did fine. Hardly any blisters and very few calluses. In other words, experience proves that as a person grows older his hands harden and his buttocks soften.

November 9

Last night, an abrupt return to reality: Sector *capsized twice. It hadn't happened to me for three weeks.*

The first time it was as if I were being given a gentle reminder. It was the least threatening capsize since I'd set out. A three-hundred-and-sixty degree revolution in the space of a few seconds. I was fast asleep when it happened. When I woke up I wasn't even sure the boat had actually capsized until I checked and found a number of objects not in their usual place. In other words, it was a real sweetheart as capsizes go. And yet, two hours later I was out in the cockpit battening down the oars, not wearing my safety harness, although the winds were high, and if the same thing had happened then — that is, if the boat had turned over and righted itself immediately — it would have sailed away leaving me in its wake. Fault me for not buckling up, but after going through a full somersault, you tend to think that lightning won't strike again right away.

Not true. Just before dawn *Sector* turned over again. I had done my best to distribute the weight throughout the trip, so that one side or the other was not too heavy, yet at this point my starboard stern was considerably heavier than

153

the port and I had all I could do, battling waves and wind, to turn over. Twenty minutes passed with no apparent progress, till finally it rolled back over. By then, I was so tired I couldn't even remember what I was supposed to do next.

November 11

Four months! A terrible night.

The boat capsized at about 2000 hours. Took me about 10–15 minutes to get it righted. I had just taken a leak and was about to empty my "chamber pot" overboard, through the open porthole. One can only imagine what might have happened if I had taken my leak a minute later!

Cold. Very cold.

I rowed under a bright moon tonight, and it was comforting to think that I might be able to enjoy the moon's company till the end of my trip. Very heavy westerly swells, waves up to twenty-five feet, though not unpleasant, since they were not breaking. But my nerves were still raw, and for all intents and purposes I could no longer sleep.

Radio conversation with a journalist, who asked me, "How far are you now from the coast?"

"More than 400 miles."

"Ah, so you can see the coastline?"

No comment.

November 12

I informed Christopher that I was aiming for the Columbia River and landfall somewhere between November 21 and 23.

Somehow frightening to have reached a fixed time and place of arrival, with no hard knowledge of the weather conditions. Final straight line. Frightening, too, to think that even this close to land anything might still happen, especially if there are squalls close to shore.

Trying to be careful, but just too exhausted, I hadn't realized that I had become crotchety, emptied out, worn down like an old man. It was high time this ordeal come to an end.

11

The "Heavenly Bum"

November 14

Eddy had provided me with some accurate weather information: two very low pressure systems were predicted for the following several days. Near the coast, where the ocean floor rose abruptly, the sea would probably prove impossible. Landing at the wrong moment could well turn into a catastrophe. I had to calculate my progress in careful doses to make sure I reached land at a propitious moment.

November 16

In the early evening, the bottom fell out of the barometer. A sort of tornado, with winds of up to sixty miles an hour, waves breaking and crisscrossing in every direction at once.

The storm passed through as quickly as it had arrived.

November 17

Christopher phoned me from the Astoria Hotel, on the Columbia River, in the state of Oregon. I asked him if he could lease a ship and a hardy crew to come out and meet me when I got close to shore. There was no way I wanted the U.S. Coast Guard to come out and pick me up if the weather got so bad I couldn't make land on my own. I wanted to remain in charge of my own destiny, and for that I needed an impeccable organization.

At the end of my conversation with Christopher, I had this rather strange reaction: "Christopher, after I arrive, can I count on you to protect me?" Despite my impatience to land, I was also afraid of having to deal with people's questions, terrified of having to talk to them. Perhaps after all this time I'd gotten used to my damn solitude?

November 18

How hard, how incredibly hard, the final phase was turning out to be. It was raining. Icy rains. Melting snow.

John Oakes, the owner of the *Miss Mary*, could not believe what he was hearing. These French are really out of their minds. Put out to sea in this weather, with winds of seventy knots and waves of thirty to thirty-five feet being predicted . . . and they come asking him to lift anchor and set out to sea to meet one of their compatriots who's arriving from Japan in a rowboat! Not surprising they can't find anyone to take them.

John is anything but timorous: he's a seasoned veteran of fishing expeditions off the Alaskan coasts, which are not exactly made for Sunday sailors. He knows how treacherous the approaches to the Columbia River can be. Miles and miles of virtually impassable reefs, a sea that is

157

indescribable during bad weather, with more than two thousand registered shipwrecks to prove it.

And to top it off, here's this guy everyone has been talking about for the last several days, a twenty-six-foot rowboat, with less than a foot of freeboard, a boat that has been out at sea for more than four months.

Taking all this into consideration, John made his decision:

"Let's get this tub moving!"

November 19

Never had the sea been worse, more difficult to navigate. In close to the shore, the currents, coupled with the gale force winds, created a monstrous riptide that ran perpendicular to the long swells of the Pacific. I had experienced rougher seas, but this was a new kind, one made to crush and pulverize, a killing sea. These waves were watery avalanches, solid masses going head to head with one another.

Christopher had told me that the fishing trawler *Miss Mary* was putting out to meet me. I found that hard to believe. In any event, even if it did manage to set sail in this weather, its chances of finding me in these seas would be the nautical equivalent of finding the needle in a haystack. But then I learned that my old pal Olivier de Kersauson* was on board the *Miss Mary*. If anyone could produce the miracle, I knew he could.

If Olivier were looking for me I knew he had to be in contact with Christopher on shore. That meant that their

* On January 25, 1993, de Kersauson and a crew of five left the French port of Brest aboard a twenty-seven meter trimaran, *Charel*. Their goal: to be the first to circumnavigate the globe in eighty days.

means of communication had to be via station KMI. For hours on end I combed the wavelengths trying to make contact, but my batteries were almost dead and I constantly came up empty. The skies had been overcast for several days, so the solar panels had not been charging at all. One or two more tries, I knew, would use up the last of my electricity.

John Oakes was at the helm of the *Miss Mary*, peering into the watery gloom, his trawler listing dangerously to port and starboard, sometimes as much as thirty to thirty-five degrees. It was also pitching like some oceangoing bronco; at times its stern rose completely out of the water and its propeller raced, churning air, the ship vibrated from stem to stern, then slammed back into the water as its bow in turn bucked upward. The next wave would submerge the deck, the spray washing over the decks and smashing up against the bridge.

The television technicians on board were cursing the fate that had forced them into this terrible position. If there was a slim chance they might get some decent pictures, maybe it would be worth it. But now, at only nine o'clock in the morning, it was still almost totally dark. In the radio room of the *Miss Mary*, Olivier refused to admit defeat. Once again he put in a call to Christopher, checking to see if by chance he had made contact with me.

"KMI, KMI, this is *Miss Mary* calling KMI. Please come in."

"Olivier, this is not KMI. This is Gerard calling. I hear you, Olivier. Do you read me?"

Apparently, the sound of my voice coming through had the effect of an electroshock on board the *Miss Mary*. I gave them my present position. John made a quick calculation of my projected movement and adjusted his heading accordingly. In ten minutes, they should be in sight.

*   *   *

159

I could barely hear the sound of *Miss Mary*'s engines over the roar of the waves and winds, but just as I did hear them a giant wave hit broadside and, once again, *Sector* was on its back. As they say, it's not over till it's over!

My antenna was underwater, therefore the radio was out of commission. I was about to start pumping, to fill the starboard ballast tank and, presumably, right the boat, when I thought to see if I could rouse Olivier on my little portable ultra-high-frequency radio, which was meant for conversations boat-to-boat at close proximity.

"Olivier, Olivier. Gerard calling. Do you read me?"

Silence. I would have to wait till I got *Sector* righted and the antenna could again start functioning.

On the bottom of the hull, which since the boat was overturned was out of the water, was a bronze plate meant to serve as a bonding jumper; it was attached to the main radio by a copper wire. On the off chance that it might work, I attached the antenna of my high-frequency radio to the copper wire, and tried calling.

"Olivier. *Miss Mary*?"

"I hear you, Gerard." The answer came in loud and clear. "Keep talking. We're homing in on your radio signal. We're almost there!"

Without question, this whole thing was turning surreal. I decided that I would refrain from righting the boat till the *Miss Mary* arrived. Hull up, *Sector* would drift more slowly.

"Gerard! Gerard! I can see you. You're no more than fifty yards away!"

And there I was — closeted in an overturned boat that was being tossed about by waves up to thirty feet high, still defying this ocean that was not going to get the better of me.

"Olivier, do you hear me? Tell them to get out their cameras. I'm going to show off now. A live demonstration,

160

right before your very eyes, of how I turn this damn thing right side up!"

Without further ado I set about shifting *Sector*'s ballast, as I had done so many times before, and like a docile little lamb *Sector* gently did a 180-degree turn and landed right-side up. What a spectacle. I was as excited as a kid with a new toy!

I called over to *Miss Mary* on my high-frequency radio and listened with swelling pride to their chorus of congratulations, which I, idiot that I am, had the gall to believe I deserved.

But the Pacific does not like braggarts or blowhards. If my private combat might have pleased this ocean, my public display of victory clearly did not. The punishment was swift and sure. *Sector* was suddenly picked up by an enormous groundswell and hurled forward at a speed of at least twenty knots; it made a forward somersault, was then knocked over on its back and turned back over again, and, before I knew what was happening, the whole process was repeated, as *Sector* did a second complete gyration.

I was flattened against the bulkhead of the cockpit, my face a bloody mess, my back a mass of shooting pains, one finger broken. The only thing that kept me from fainting was the pain.

Sector, which I had finally concluded was indestructible, was not in much better shape than I was. There was a crack in the cabin deck at least twenty inches long. And to make sure the lesson was driven home, in the unlikely event it had not gotten through to me, or that I had perhaps not taken it to heart, no one on the decks of the *Miss Mary* had seen a thing; no one had even the slightest indication that something was wrong. All they had seen was the enormous white mass that had picked me up and vomited me out a few hundred yards away.

*   *   *

An hour later, the person who appeared before the passengers and crew of the *Miss Mary* was an old man, a creature both haggard and wild-eyed whom Kersauson would later refer to as "the heavenly bum." That person looked at these spectators for a long, long time without saying a word, then burst into tears.

November 19, 1900 hours

The weather had improved, but the seas were still heavy as I resumed rowing. The *Miss Mary* headed back, bearing with her the Dantesque pictures that the television crews had taken of me earlier. By now, I suspected, they were being shown on television sets the world over. In a few hours, my crossing would no longer be mine alone.

November 20, 1800 hours

The *Miss Mary* was following me a short distance away. On board, I could see a lot of commotion. I was able to pick out Kersauson and saw that he was pointing to something behind me.

Yes, Olivier, I know, I know. But leave me alone for a few more hours, a few minutes at least; I have to pull my thoughts together. . . .

A hundred. All I wanted was to count up to a hundred. A hundred strokes, a hundred gentle strokes, the most voluptuous of the entire crossing, in perfect time with the movement of the waves . . . 99 . . . 100!

I stood up on my seat and looked around. There, directly

before me, was the coastline, the wonderful, mountainous coastline, looming clearly on the horizon.

The prison door swung slowly open, but ever so slightly. . . .

From the *Miss Mary*, they passed down a bottle of Bordeaux and a real glass. I had landed in heaven!

Despite the heavy swells, the weather was not bad, but Olivier's description of the entrance of the Columbia River was less than encouraging. The waters of the river, whose currents are among the strongest of any river in North America, ran into the groundswells of the Pacific at the river's mouth and engaged in a mighty combat. Sandbanks surrounded the harbor channels, which were sheltered by reefs that in bad weather were insurmountable and in good could be crossed but only in a very narrow fairway.

Depending on the time of day and the tide, strong currents could raise the level of the sea very suddenly. What was more, the powerful river currents would be working against me because they flowed westward; my progress would be slow, extremely slow, limited to a few hours a day, during which the force of the rising tide would manage to reverse the current. According to the most recent weather reports, we had about twelve hours of good weather ahead of us — a gift we could not turn down.

I made my decision almost immediately. A sailor's decision. I would row right up to the reefs, then pass a rope to the *Miss Mary* and have it tow *Sector* through the danger zone.

I alone had laid down the rules for my crossing: row across the Northern Pacific in complete autonomy. I could, if I wanted to add to the panache, up the stakes and try to reach land myself before the bad weather set in. It was a gamble, not only extremely dangerous for me but also risky for all those who — now that I was in their waters and under their jurisdiction — would be obliged to come out to save me if I ran into trouble: the U.S. Coast Guard. I have said it before, and I think I have amply demonstrated that I practice what I preach: I was willing to put my life on the line, but I had no intention of risking the lives of others.

So the decision was made.

I took out my log, that silent companion who, since the morning over four months ago in Choshi, Japan, had been the patient witness to my laconic observations, and made my final entry.

November 21, 1415 hours.

Passed a towline to the Miss Mary *to enter the harbor channels of the Columbia River.*

I was fully aware that on board a boat prowling not far off were people who were waiting for the first light of dawn so they could take pictures of *Sector* in tow. I frankly didn't care. The sea has its own rules, which are not those of the circus.

One journalist would write: "He didn't really cross the Pacific. . . ." Who knows, maybe he was right.

In the morning the towline broke. The sea was relatively calm, even if there were still persistent groundswells. I took out the oars and resumed rowing.

Oliver came out to join *Sector* aboard a Zodiac-model sailboat and urged me to cast another line to the *Miss Mary* and let myself be towed in, since the tide was about to

164

head out. He also pointed seaward to the huge breakers off to starboard. Just imagine, he argued, what they would be like if the winds got any worse. The weather reports were not encouraging: to allow oneself to be caught in this stretch of sea could be a catastrophe.

While Olivier and I were talking, I noted that a large number of boats had joined us. Several of them were signaling to me, telling me to listen to my radio. I obliged, and from a helicopter hovering overhead, I heard my father's voice. Then it was Guillaume's, so choked up he could barely talk.

12

One Second Longer . . .

The sun, which had seemed no longer to exist, reappeared. A bird passed overhead, a odd-looking bird with ridiculously short wings. Ah, a land bird. Off to starboard, a little leaf was swimming, and I took care not to touch it with the blade of my oar as I passed by. A butterfly contemplated alighting on *Sector*, then changed its mind and flew off. Speaking of *Sector*, I knew that something was wrong: my boat had become light, so extraordinarily light.

And then I realized it actually hadn't: I had been dreaming, there must be something strange. . . .

Say, I hadn't noticed, the shoreline had moved in, the steep, sloping riverbanks were covered with Oregon pines, a lot like the shores of the Aurey River not far from Kérantré. Then, as in any dream, the most unexpected characters began to appear. To give the illusion of being real, they were setting out on various boats. A while ago it was Bernard. And there were Professor Boissonas and Dr. Chauve. Look, there was one of my sisters, and, over there, someone who looked like François, talking to Louis-Noël. . . . And a whole host of others — what a nice group! They were holding a sign that said WELCOME TO ILWACO. What an odd name! They looked as if they were having a celebration;

166

no, that wasn't quite right. They were all looking at something, as if they were trying to understand. . . .

Strange, this dream, with all those people and all those colors. Make sure to take a close look, so that when I woke up, if I hadn't forgotten, I would write all this down in my log. What a great collection of memories to be savored tomorrow morning, when it was time to start rowing, alone once again, with my mind in need of a fresh supply of images. . . .

I had the feeling I was rowing into a dead end. The water was so smooth, I had to be sleeping really soundly, I had to be far away, very far away from reality; this hadn't happened to me in a long time. How long would it be before I would suddenly be jerked awake by the pull of the sea anchor, by a slightly larger wave than usual, which would break the spell? Or, indeed, had the Pacific granted me a truce; had it at long last taken pity on me?

If this dream had really been perfect — but wasn't that asking too much? — it would also have Cornélia, Guillaume, and Ann all standing there, at the edge of the dock.

As for me, I was going to glide in to a silent landing, without uttering a word. I would remove my sticky slicker, take off my foul-smelling boots, put my oars back carefully where they belonged. I would try to gain some time, but above all I would make no sudden movement that might wake me up from this dream, this dream in which I felt so good, wanting to make it last a little longer, just one second longer. An eternity.